The Observer's Pocket Series

GARDEN FLOWERS

Observer's Books

NATURAL HISTORY

Birds · Birds' Eggs · Wild Animals · Zoo Animals
Farm Animals · Freshwater Fishes · Sea Fishes
Tropical Fishes · Butterflies · Larger Moths
Insects and Spiders · Pond Life · Sea and Seashore
Seashells · Dogs · Horses and Ponies · Cats
Trees · Wild Flowers · Grasses · Mushrooms
Lichens · Cacti · Garden Flowers · Flowering Shrubs
House Plants · Vegetables · Geology · Weather
Astronomy

SPORT

Association Football · Cricket · Golf · Coarse Fishing
Fly Fishing · Show Jumping · Motor Sport

TRANSPORT

Automobiles · Aircraft · Commercial Vehicles
Motorcycles · Steam Locomotives · Ships
Small Craft · Manned Spaceflight
Unmanned Spaceflight

ARCHITECTURE

Architecture · Churches · Cathedrals

COLLECTING

Awards and Medals · Coins · Postage Stamps
Glass · Pottery and Porcelain · Furniture

ARTS AND CRAFTS

Music · Painting · Modern Art · Sculpture
Sewing

HISTORY AND GENERAL INTEREST

Ancient Britain · Flags · Heraldry
European Costume

TRAVEL

London · Tourist Atlas GB

The Observer's Book of

GARDEN FLOWERS

compiled by

DAVID PYCRAFT

based on the larger work
THE BOOK OF GARDEN FLOWERS
by G. A. R. Phillips

WITH 150 ILLUSTRATIONS IN COLOUR
BY JOAN LUPTON

FREDERICK WARNE

LONDON

Published by
Frederick Warne (Publishers) Ltd

LIBRARY OF CONGRESS CATALOG
CARD NO. 74–806121

ISBN 0 7232 1531 6

Printed in Great Britain by
William Clowes & Sons, Limited
London, Beccles and Colchester

1650.377

CONTENTS

PREFACE

The basic aim of this pocket-sized book is to help the gardener in choosing plants for the flower garden—plants that will grow well under most conditions, give a good display of bloom and, in many cases, provide cut flowers for house decoration.

The introduction in recent years of many new hybrid strains and improved forms, has inevitably led to a reduction in the number of species grown by nurserymen. Many plants mentioned in earlier editions of this book are no longer easily obtainable, although they may still be occasionally offered by specialist nurserymen or seen in botanic gardens, or in gardens of old country houses. Thus, in selecting plants for the one hundred and fifty pages of descriptive text, and keeping in mind the need to include primarily plants readily obtainable as plants or seed from leading nurserymen, bulb growers or seedsmen, some infrequently encountered kinds have been retained to give the reader some insight into the diversity of size, form and colour within genera now perhaps represented in our gardens by a single species. In all instances varieties and forms mentioned are considered to be among the best of those readily available.

Roses are not included, nor, with a few exceptions, are shrubby plants or rock garden plants—all large plant groups needing individual attention. But flowering plants for all seasons are included, from the snowdrop of still-dark winter days to the Michaelmas daisy of late autumn.

Miss Joan Lupton's charming illustrations will greatly help identification, and a flowering and planting table has been included for easy reference, together with notes on cultivation and control of pests and diseases.

The subjects are arranged in alphabetical order under species names. The scope of the volume can be seen at a glance by referring to the list of contents on page 5.

A note on the use of names in text and index: family names are printed in capitals, e.g. COMPOSITAE, species names in italics, e.g. *Bellis perennis*, common names in roman type, e.g. snowdrop. Varietal names appear in quotation marks, e.g. 'Rob Roy'. Where space allows, synonyms and common names have been included.

It is hoped that with the help of this book the reader will get to know many of his garden plants a little better, and in doing so find both pleasure and benefit.

INTRODUCTION

Herbaceous Perennials

Herbaceous Perennials are plants which do not develop wood tissue as do shrubs. Their foliage and stems die back to ground level at the end of the growing season each year, but food is stored in a variety of underground parts—fleshy roots, bulbs, tubers, etc.—and thus the plants are perpetuated, growth resuming again each spring.

Planting Where the soil is light and well-drained, autumn planting—late September to late October—will enable plants to become established while the soil still holds summer warmth. They will then have the advantage of renewing growth in spring as established plants. Where however the soil is heavy, autumn planting may lead to overwinter losses if the soil becomes wet and waterlogged. On such soils it is better to defer planting until March or April, when the soil is again workable with the arrival of milder spring weather. Hollow-stemmed plants such as delphiniums, and all grey or silver-foliaged plants are best planted in spring.

Bulbous plants which flower in late winter or early spring, such as crocus, grape hyacinth and scillas, should be planted in late summer or early autumn, September being the ideal month. Exceptions are daffodils which, being early-rooting, are best planted by the end of August, tulips which can be planted up to November, and snowdrops best planted or moved immediately after flowering when in full leaf. Gladioli and other summer-flowering bulbous plants from warm climates require planting in April or early May. Being somewhat tender, if planted too early they may, as they emerge, be damaged by late frosts. For early flowering, gladioli can be planted in pots in autumn, and grown on in gentle warmth for planting out in May.

Out-door chrysanthemums are usually sold as pot-grown young plants already hardened off for immediate planting out of doors in April. Dahlias can be obtained as dormant tubers, or as leafly young pot-grown plants, again usually hardened off and less troublesome than dormant tubers. The tubers must be lifted, cleaned, carefully dried and stored, with other non-hardy bulbous plants, as soon as possible after the first autumn frost. Tubers should be stored until required in boxes of dry soil or sand in cool dry conditions, temperature preferably about 4° C (40° F), boxing up and bringing into gentle warmth from early April onwards. They must be hardened off carefully and not planted out until late May or early June, when all risk of frost is past.

Site An important factor in growing perennials well is choice of site. The majority prefer a well-drained soil and a sunny position—or at least sun for a considerable period each day. Choose a sunny site if possible. In the past, long hedge, wall or fence-backed borders were the rule, taller plants at the back inevitably being drawn forwards towards the light and needing considerable extra attention to staking. A more labour-saving approach is to plant in island beds, choosing sturdy or compact kinds which can be grown free-standing, needing no support. Many perennials will grow well in the shade of trees provided conditions are moist and the shade is not too dense. In the deep shade of densely-leafy trees, where the soil is dry, very few plants will grow successfully. In choosing perennials for various parts of the garden always take into consideration the growing conditions and limitations of each site.

Soil Preparation As perennials—with the exception of bulbs—are usually left undisturbed for at least 3 years, thorough preparation of the site is essential. Firstly attend to drainage if the site is subject to waterlogging and no other site is available. If there is a deep layer of top-soil, double-digging would be advantageous. If not well-manured in the past, incorporate a good dressing of well-rotted organic material during digging. Well-rotted farmyard manure is the best material to use, but is now difficult to obtain, and materials such as well-made garden compost, leaf-mould or peat can be used, supplemented with an organic fertilizer such as equal parts bonemeal and hoof and horn meal at the rate of 3 to 4 ounces per sq. yard. Sphagnum moss peat is an excellent improver of all soils, improving the moisture-retentive qualities of lighter soils and, used with sharp sand, grit or weathered ash, the workability of heavy clay soils. It is, however, necessary to ensure that the peat is moist before use; if dry, break up well and thoroughly soak. This can be done quite easily by putting the peat into sacks, weighting down with bricks, then immersing overnight in a bath or tub of rain water.

In double-digging a trench is excavated to a spade's-depth at one end of the strip to be dug, the excavated soil being transported to the other end of the strip to be used to fill in the final trench. The bottom of the first trench is forked over, then the next spit (spade's depth) turned over, leaving a second trench. The process is repeated over the length of the strip, well-rotted organic matter being dug well in with the top spit or spread along the bottom of each trench after forking. With island beds or broad borders divide into two sections for digging, starting and finishing at the same end of the plot, and thus obviating the necessity of transporting soil from one end of the plot to the other. If the soil is shallow, over gravel or chalk, dig shallowly. Do not mix fertile topsoil with underlying infertile soil or materials. Do not dig and plant in one operation. Allow several weeks for the soil to settle before planting. In digging, remove all pieces of roots of perennial weeds such as couch grass and bindweed. Perennial weeds are extremely difficult to eradicate amongst herbaceous perennials, where use of weedkillers is limited to the very careful dipping of shoots of weeds, such as bindweed, in solutions of one of the growth-regulating weedkillers used for lawn weed control. This is effective in time, but rather tedious, usually requiring repeated treatment over two or more seasons.

Most perennials prefer a neutral soil, neither acid nor alkaline, although many grow naturally on chalky soils. There are various soil test kits available with which one can easily ascertain whether the soil is excessively acid, remedying if necessary with a dressing of ground chalk or ground limestone, applying in winter immediately after digging and allowing it to be washed in by the rain. A few perennials dislike lime, particularly some lilies.

Planting A few days before planting lightly tread, then rake in a dressing of a complete fertilizer (known also as general or balanced fertilizer) at about 3 oz. per sq. yard. Mark out planting positions in advance, then lay out and plant carefully but quickly to avoid roots drying out. Firm well.

Maintenance During the first growing season after planting, artificial watering may be needed as the root systems of the plants will not be fully established. When watering, soak thoroughly. In subsequent years an annual mulch of compost, peat of leaf-mould as growth begins in the spring will help to conserve moisture, but it may be necessary to irrigate if growth is slow to develop in very dry spring conditions. A dressing of a complete fertilizer can be applied annually in spring, where necessary, before mulching.

Taller-growing plants or those with lax habit may need supporting. The best support for most plants is birch or hazel brushwood, pushed firmly into the soil around and through the various clumps, bending over the top 30 cm or so to form a framework through which the plants will grow and flower. This should be done when growth is about 30 cm high. Vigorous growth will quickly hide the brushwood support—which should be varied in height according to the height of the plants to be supported. Individual canes can be used to support plants such as gladioli, lilies and delphiniums, but a better method, giving more flexible support, is to insert three or four canes around each clump, encircling with twine at intervals, making a light, framelike structure. Dahlias can be given similar, but sturdier, support.

Weeds should be kept down by frequent light hoeing. This is particularly important in the early weeks after planting. When growth has been killed back by the first keen autumn frosts, cut back growth to ground level, then clean beds and lightly fork over. After three or four years, borders tend to become overcrowded, the balance between groups being lost through dominance of stronger-growing kinds. At this stage one can reorganize, removing less suitable kinds and introducing new ones.

Propagation With the establishment of a few plants it is a simple matter to increase one's stock. There are three basic methods of propagation:

(1) *Seed* A natural method of reproduction of all flowering plants. The seed of species will usually produce plants fairly true to type with little variation from one generation to another. Some garden forms may also reproduce fairly true to type but others, including hybrids, may show considerable variation in form and colour. Thus, to perpetuate selected forms it is usually necessary to propagate by division or from cuttings. Hybrids must always be propagated by these means. F1 hybrids, increasingly listed in seed catalogues, are the offspring resulting from crossing two carefully selected parent plants each having certain desirable characteristics, colour, size, etc., the offspring showing the combined good qualities of both parents and the vigour which many hybrids possess. Being hybrids, collected seed from these plants will not come true. The raisers must repeat the cross each season using the original parents. F2 hybrids, whilst showing the good qualities of F1 hybrids, tend to be more variable in their characteristics.

Seed viability (life) varies considerably. Seed of some plants may remain viable for 5 to 10 years or more if suitably stored. With others, particularly bulbous plants, unless the seed is sown in autumn as soon as ripe, few if any seed may germinate the following spring. Seed of most hardy plants can, however, be stored overwinter in cool dry conditions and sown in April in well-prepared seedbeds in the open. One can in fact continue to collect and sow seed as it ripens during spring and summer, up to September. A method which usually gives good results, particularly with bulbous plant seeds, is to sow in pots or pans in September, using John Innes seed compost and following the basic technique described for half-hardy annuals up to the seed-sowing stage. Then cover the seed with a centimetre layer of sharp grit before placing out of doors in a cool position out of direct sun, such as at the foot of a north-facing wall. Plunge the containers to the rim in a bed of weathered ash or similar porous material to conserve moisture. Cover with fine mesh wire-netting to protect from birds or mice. In early March transference to gentle warmth may encourage germination. If not, return out of doors and keep undisturbed for at least a further twelve months.

Seed of plants from milder climates, such as gladioli and African lilies (*Agapanthus*), will usually germinate better if sown in warmth in late January or February, or under a cold frame or cloches in March. Treat woodland primulas and meconopsis similarly. Transplant seedlings to boxes when large enough to handle, harden off carefully, then plant out when danger of frost is past.

(2) *Division* The easiest method of propagating all clump-forming perennials. Clumps are lifted and broken up by hand with the help of a knife, or using two forks back to back. The central worn-out parts are discarded, retaining small sections of healthy outer growth. This is done during the normal planting periods. Early spring-flowering plants are best divided in autumn; bearded iris immediately after flowering. Paeonies are best left undisturbed but, i moving is essential, move in autumn as the foliage be- gins to die down, carefully dividing before replanting into small sections each comprising a large healthy tuber with one or two strong buds showing at th neck.

(3) *Cuttings* Chrysanthemums, dahlias and del phiniums are raised commercially in large quantitie from stem cuttings. Phlox, which could easily b

propagated by division, is increased by cuttings to avoid transmitting eelworm, a serious pest which infests the roots of the plant. Other perennials can be similarly propagated. The cuttings are taken in early spring of the new growths when they are 5 to 7·5 cm long. They are taken just below a node or, in the case of dahlias, with a small piece of tuber attached. After trimming lower leaves and dipping the base in a rooting powder (not essential but aids good rooting) the cuttings are inserted in pots or boxes in a good rooting medium, such as 2 parts sharp horticultural sand to 1 part sieved peat, watered in and placed in a propagating frame, preferably with warmth for chrysanthemums and dahlias. Pot on when well rooted, hardening off if necessary before planting out. August or September is the best period to take cuttings of perennials unlikely to survive an average winter out of doors, e.g. heliotrope, geraniums (zonal pelargoniums), penstemons; potting up when well-rooted and keeping in a cool or frost-free greenhouse or frame over winter. Cuttings of shrubby plants mentioned in this book are best taken in late June to early August, short lengths of half-ripened new growths taken just below a node being treated as for hardy perennials, warmth being required to ensure good rooting.

Root cuttings Plants that have thick, fleshy roots, such as oriental poppy, can be propagated easily from short sections of the thicker roots. These are taken in late winter or early spring, each about 2·5 cm long, inserting vertically in boxes or pots of sandy compost, covering with about a 1-cm layer of sand and watering in well, then treating as for stem cuttings.

Bulbous Plants These are usually propagated by means of offsets which form around the base of the bulb. When the parent bulbs are lifted after the leaves have died down, these are removed and planted in rows in a nursery bed. Gladioli will often produce numerous corms in this manner. They can be stored overwinter in sand and planted out at the normal time.

Annual Plants

An annual plant is one which completes its life-cycle—from germination of seed, to flowering and the development of new seed, after which the plant dies—within a single growing season.

Hardy Annuals (**HA**) These are plants which will tolerate a considerable degree of frost, and seedlings or young plants wili not be seriously harmed by late spring frosts. Thus they can be sown out of doors in early spring where the plants are to flower. The usual period for sowing is late March or April, when the sun is gaining strength, the soil is warming and is easily workable—not frozen or heavy with rain. In the south, and on lighter soils, one can sow earlier than in the north and on heavier clayey soils where conditions are usually less favourable for early sowing. Seeds that are sown in unfavourable conditions may fail to germinate or give a very poor germination rate.

In unfavourable areas seed can be sown under glass in February, the seedlings being pricked into boxes and grown on, hardening off in a cold frame for planting out of doors in May. Those kinds that do not transplant well can be sown two or three seeds to a small pot and thinned at the seedling stage to leave the strongest seedling only. The main drawback with this method is that it utilizes greenhouse or frame space which might be needed for tender plants.

Quite a number of hardy annuals can be sown in late August or early September from freshly collected seed, e.g. cornflowers, larkspur, nigella. Provided one guards against attack by slugs, this method will provide sturdy young plants for early flowering the following spring. Results may be poor, depending on seasonal conditions, on very dry soils or those prone to waterlogging.

Half-hardy Annuals (**HHA**) A grouping of plants, usually of tropical or subtropical origin, mostly perennial in habit and having little tolerance of frost, e.g. lobelias, tobacco plants (*Nicotiana*), verbena. In Britain they are usually grown as annuals, flowering over a long period in summer and autumn. They can be sown out of doors in May when there is little danger of severe weather, but will usually not reach a reasonable flowering size until late in the year, except perhaps in favourable seasons and mild areas. Therefore they are normally sown in a heated greenhouse in early spring—February to April—sowing in a sterilized soil-based seed compost such as the standard John Innes seed compost. The formula for this is two parts by bulk medium loam (sifted, friable, containing little or no sand), 1 part by bulk granulated sphagnum moss peat, 1 part by bulk sharp clean sand, plus 1½ oz. superphosphate and ¾ oz. ground chalk or ground limestone per bushel of compost. If making up one's own compost, sterilization of the loam is essential to destroy any harmful organisms present and to kill weed seeds—which otherwise may germinate at the same time as the annuals. Various small electrical sterilizers are available for amateur use. Small quantities of loam can be sterilized by heating the soil to 82° to 93° C (180° to 200° F) in a metal container inside a larger saucepan half filled with water. Maintain temperature for 30 minutes, then spread thinly on a clean surface to cool rapidly before use.

Sow seed thinly in shallow seed pans, pots or seed boxes. Press compost down firmly, allowing space for watering seedlings prior to pricking out. Cover seed lightly with sifted soil unless seed packet instructions advise otherwise. Prick out seedlings into boxes when large enough to handle, and grow on under glass, hardening off in a cold frame or sheltered corner for 2 to 3 weeks before planting out, when there is little further danger of frost—mid-May to early June. Zinnias are best grown individually in pots, from the seed-stage prior to bedding out. Salvias and others can also be raised in pots where good specimens are required for spot planting in bedding schemes. After planting out, water thoroughly.

Tender Annuals A third category of annuals comprises those which thrive out of doors only in the warmer days of summer. Best described as tender annuals, they include calceolaria and schizanthus. They are usually grown as pot plants for greenhouse or conservatory, and can be bedded out in late June/early July to add interest and colour to borders or bedding displays, but results may be poor in a cold wet summer.

Hardy Perennials grown as Annuals A number of perennials are grown as annuals, e.g. Californian poppy (*Eschscholtzia*), foxglove, as flowering after the first season is seldom satisfactory. There are also annual species or strains of quite a number of popular perennials, e.g. chrysanthemum, coreopsis, lupin.

Tender Shrubby Perennials grown as Annuals A number of woody perennials, native to warmer climates, such as heliotrope and zonal pelargoniums (commonly called geraniums) which will flower well out of doors if the summer is favourable. They will not, however, survive our winters out of doors. Plants can be kept overwinter in the greenhouse, but can take up considerable space and, as young plants almost invariably are better in appearance and performance, young plants are usually raised annually from seed or cuttings, treating as for half-hardy annuals.

Hardy Biennials These are plants which differ from annuals in that they require two seasons of growth to complete their life-cycles—a period of warmth for growth, followed by a period of cooler conditions to induce flowering. Well-known examples are Brompton stock, Canterbury bell and honesty. A number of perennials are commonly grown as biennials, e.g. hollyhock, sweet william, wallflower. Seed of all biennials should be sown in May or June, sowing thinly in drills 15 to 22 cm apart, ensuring the soil is kept adequately moist during germination and seedling growth. When large enough to handle, prick out seedlings in good fertile soil. The resultant sturdy plants are transplanted to their flowering positions in early autumn, flowering the following spring or early summer.

Soil Preparation and Outdoor Sowing Siting of annuals is important, most being sun-lovers. The site should preferably be south-facing or receive sun for a good part of the day. Avoid exposed situations where taller plants may be buffeted by strong winds and rain. A few annuals, such as tobacco plants and stocks, are tolerant of semi-shade or sunless situations.

Annuals may be used in various ways—in window-boxes, hanging baskets or tubs, in small groups in perennial or mixed borders, or as space-fillers in a variety of situations. Where space allows, a border entirely of annuals will give colour over many weeks but, in the case of hardy annuals, will involve a considerable amount of work in seed-bed preparation, seed sowing, seedling thinning and careful weeding.

The soil for annuals should not be too rich or heavily manured as this can result in too lush foliage and few flowers. A light dry soil can, however, be improved by working in a dressing of moisture-retentive peat or leaf-mould, a heavy soil lightened by incorporating sharp sand or grit. If fertility is thought to be poor, apply a complete fertilizer at 3 ounces per sq. yard about 10 days before sowing or planting. Seed is best sown in shallow parallel drills some centimetres apart, first marking out the area into irregular-shaped patches, a different annual being sown in each patch. Vary the angle of drills from one patch to another. Some patches can be planted later with half-hardy annuals. Sow thinly and cover lightly. Weed and hoe carefully between the rows with a hand hoe as soon as seedlings are easily distinguishable. Thin as soon as well-established to 10 to 15 cm, if necessary thinning later to final spacings (instructions are usually given on seed packet). Autumn-sown annuals are best thinned in late autumn to no more than 5 cm apart as a precaution against winter losses from slugs, etc., thinning again as growth begins in spring. Taller-growing plants may need a little brushwood support (see perennial section for method recommended).

Insects, Pests and Diseases

Both annuals and perennials may suffer considerable damage from insect attack and from disease. While identification of harmful insects and disease symptoms is frequently a matter for the specialist, the observant gardener may often be able to identify a trouble and take appropriate steps to control it.

Insects and Pests Where a new garden is being constructed on a site previously grassland, there is considerable initial risk of attack from soil-living pests such as chafer grubs, cutworms, leather-jackets and wireworms. Thorough cultivation will, however, bring many of these to the surface where they will be eaten by birds.

Slugs and snails, feeding at night, can quickly destroy young seedlings and badly damage plants that have been newly bedded out. They are attracted by decaying organic matter or by plant debris. If troublesome, avoid using rich farm or animal manures, or garden compost as surface mulches, and clear any plant debris, leaves, etc., accumulating in odd corners, destroying any slugs or slug eggs encountered.

Leaf-eating caterpillars can cause serious damage if not checked at the first signs of attack. Frequent hand-picking, although tedious, is a useful approach; birds will also reduce infestations.

Sap-sucking greenfly and other aphids weaken plants, distort growth and may spread virus. Here, too, birds will often reduce infestations.

Eelworms, microscopic creatures, can be troublesome on a number of herbaceous plants, particularly perennial phlox and chrysanthemums. Where possible, plant only reliable healthy stock obtained from reputable sources. Do not propagate from plants which appear to be unhealthy.

Insecticides The amateur can usually maintain a good degree of control over greenfly and other sap-sucking insects by regular use of derris or pyrethrum-based sprays, both widely used for many years, and over caterpillars by using derris in powder form.

Greenfly can even be deterred to some extent simply by spraying with soapy water.

Diseases These can also be troublesome, particularly among bedding and bulbous plants, which are very susceptible to infection by soil-borne disease organisms. These fungi build up in the soil when plants of the same type are grown in a bed several years running and they attack the roots of bulbs, causing rotting, so that affected plants collapse. Such troubles can be prevented by growing different types of bedding and bulbous plants each season.

Several different fungi can cause powdery mildew on herbaceous plants, but all show as a white powdery coating on leaves, shoots and occasionally flowers. They can be prevented to a great extent by mulching and irrigating in hot weather before the soil dries out completely. Affected plants can be sprayed at 10 to 14 day intervals with a copper fungicide. Rust diseases are unsightly and difficult to control. Resistant varieties of antirrhinums should be grown. New hollyhock plants should be raised every second year. Viruses cause stunting of plants and distortion, mottling and striping of leaves and flowers. Affected plants should be burned.

The damping off of seedlings under glass is usually due to attacks by soil-borne fungi. To avoid this risk sterilized soil should always be used and boxes of seedlings given a watering with Cheshunt Compound.

The success of control measures depends on correct diagnosis, and where there is any doubt, specialist advice should always be sought.

GLOSSARY

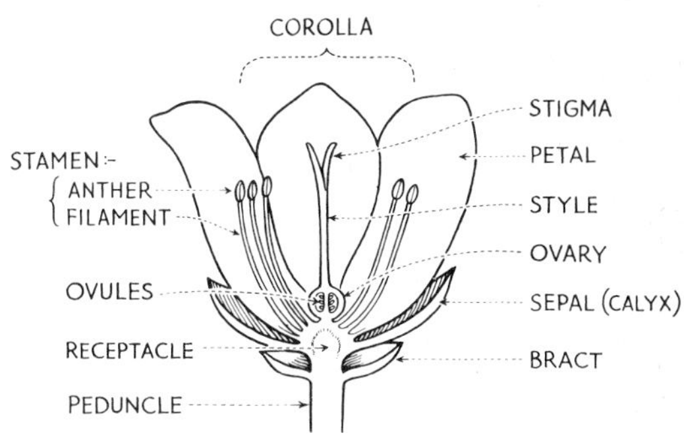

Section of Flower

Alternate succeeding regularly on opposite sides of a branch.

Annual plants which flower and die in the same year as they are raised from seed.

Anther the male organ of a flowering plant, the head of the stamen.

Arrow-shaped Leaf a wide base with two pointed lobes directed downwards.

Axil the angle between a stem and the upper side of a leaf-stalk.

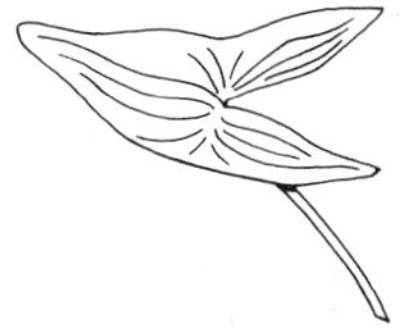

Arrow Shaped

Basal leaves at the base of a plant.

Biennial plants which flower in the year following that in which the seeds are sown, after which they die.

Bigeneric a cross between two species of different genera.
Botryoid like a bunch of grapes.
Bract a modified leaf beneath a flower.
Bracteole a diminutive bract.
Bulbil a small bulb attached to the main bulb.

Bract

Calyx the cup or collection of sepals of a flower.
Campanulate bell-shaped.
Capitulum a close cluster of flowers consisting of tiny florets packed together on a common platform.
Carpel a division of the ovary or seed vessel.
Clasping Leaf when a stalkless leaf encircles the stem.
Cleistogene flowers devoid of a corolla. The flowers never open, but develop into fruits by self-fertilization.
Compound a leaf broken up into several leaflets.
Connate when the bases of opposite leaves are grown together.
Cordate heart-shaped.
Corm a bulbous underground stem.
Corolla the inner whorl of the flower composed of the petals.
Corona the outer edge of a radiated compound flower.

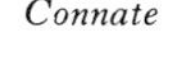
Connate

Corymb where the cluster of flowers is brought more or less to the same level.
Cruciferous with four petals in the form of a cross.
Cyme a shoot terminating in a flower, then sending off side branches each of which terminate in like manner.

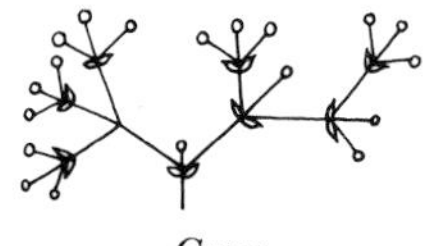
Cyme

Deciduous plants and trees which shed their leaves in winter.
Decumbent lying flat (usually with tip raised).
Digitate Leaf leaflets radiating from the leaf-stalk.
Dimorphic flowers that appear in two forms such as the Primrose, in which one form has a short style with anthers near the mouth of the corolla-tube, and the other form has a long style and anthers midway down the tube.

Disc the central part of a radiate flower in which the florets are tubular.

Entire Leaf having the margin undivided.

Ericaceous belonging to the heath family.

Filament the stalk-like portion of the stamen.

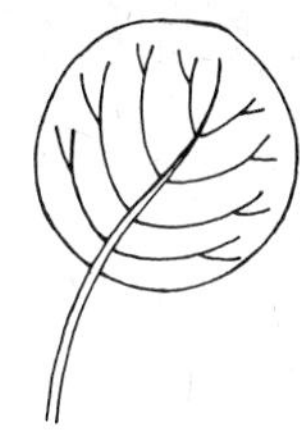

Entire leaf

Florescence the blossoming of a plant; the flowering season.

Floret one of the small flowers in a composite blossom; a floweret.

Floriferous bearing flowers.

Funicle a small stalk by which the seed is attached to the placenta.

Genera the plural of *genus.*

Genus an assemblage of species, which all agree in one or more important structural character.

Glaucous a sea-green colour; having a down of this colour.

Heart-shaped Leaf broad, with two rounded lobes.

Hybridized produced from two species.

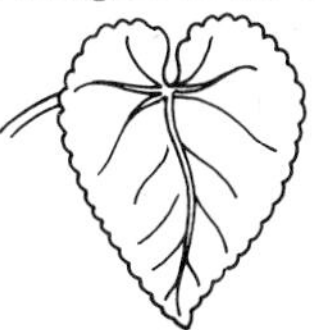

Heart-shaped

Hypogynous when petals or stamens spring from beneath the base of the ovary and are not attached to the calyx.

Inferior denotes that the calyx or corolla is free from and below the ovary.

Inflorescence the arrangement of grouping of the flowers on a plant; collective blossoms.

Involucre a series of bract-like leaves below a cluster of flowers.

Involucre

Keel the lowest petal of a flower, resembling the wings of a butterfly.

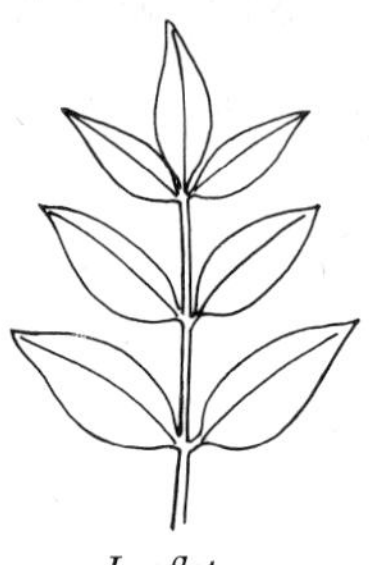
Leaflets

Laciniated with a fringed border.
Lanceolate gradually tapering towards the tip; lance-shaped.
Latifoliate having broad leaves.
Leaflets when there are several succeeding leaves on each side of a midrib; a little leaf.
Leguminous bearing seeds which split into halves like the pea.
Linear slender, a leaf that is long and very narrow with parallel sides.
Lobe a division of a leaf.

Monocarpic annual plant, or one which dies after it has once borne fruit.
Moraine accumulation of stones in a rockery simulating debris left behind by a receding glacier.

Oblong leaf

Nectary the gland of a flower which holds the nectar.
Node the point of juncture of leaf and stem.
Nodule a small knot or rounded lump.

Oval leaves

Oblong Leaf twice as long as broad with both ends rounded.
Obovate egg-shaped with the small end at the base: inversely ovate.
Offset a shoot; a short runner bending up at the end to form a new plant.
Order a group of families all of which agree in some striking particular.
Oval Leaves tapering to each end.
Ovary the seed vessel.
Ovate egg-shaped.
Ovula the seed of a plant before it is fertilized.

Palmate in the shape of a hand.

Panicle when the pedicels are branched, supporting two or more flowers in a loose cluster.

Panicle

Pappus the calyx of composite flowers; usually a whorl of bristles or silky hairs.

Pedicel a flower-stalk supporting several flowers without footstalks.

Peduncle the stalk of a flower or a cluster of flowers.

Pendent hanging down.

Pendulous hanging so as to swing.

Perennial rootstocks that increase and expand yearly.

Perfoliate Leaf when the stem passes through the base of a stalkless leaf.

Perfoliate leaf

Perianth flowers showing no distinction from calyx and corolla; the floral envelope or outer part of a flower.

Petals flower-leaves forming part of a corolla.

Petiole a leaf-stalk.

Pinnate leaflets of elongate shape, forming pairs on opposite sides.

Pistil the seed-bearing part of a flower comprising the ovary, stigma and style.

Placenta the part of the ovary to which the ovules are attached.

Pollen the fertilizing powder or male elements held by the anthers by contact of which the ovules are fertilized.

Pollinium containing pollen.

Pubescent hairy; downy.

Raceme flowers arranged like a spike but with footstalks.

Radiate a composite flower consisting of a disc in which the florets are tubular.

Radical Leaves leaves that rise directly from the rootstock.

Ray the outer part of a compound radiate flower.

Receptacle the fleshy head of the peduncle supporting the flower.

Raceme

Recurved curving outwards.

Reflex bent or turned back.

Rhizome an underground creeping stem which sends out shoots above and roots below.

Rosette rose-shaped.

Scape a flower-stalk rising direct from the rootstock.
Sepal a leaf of the calyx; the outer whorl of the perianth.
Serrated notched on the edge like a saw.
Sessile leaves or flowers connected with the stem without footstalks.
Simple Leaf an undivided leaf.
Spadix an inflorescence where the flowers are arranged round a thick fleshy spike.
Spathe the large bract that envelops certain flowers before opening.
Species individual plants bearing certain characters in common.
Spike bearing a number of flowers without footstalks.
Spreading when the petals of a flower are at right angles with the central column.
Spur a projection, usually the nectary.
Stamen the male pollen-bearing organ.
Stigma the organ holding the pollen grains at the top of the pistil.
Stipules small leaves, always in pairs at the base of a leaf-stalk.
Stolon a trailing stem which roots and develops a new plant at intervals.
Style the support for the stigma.
Succulent with fleshy foliage and stalks.

Simple leaf

Spike

Stipules

Terminal flowers produced at the summit of a stem or end of a branch.
Tomentose downy or cottony.
Trefoil a form of leaf with three leaflets.
Tuber thickened underground stem.
Tubercle a small swelling or knob.
Tuberous consisting of round fleshy tubers.

Trefoil

Umbels a flat-topped cluster of flowers having their footstalks of nearly equal length and radiating outwards.

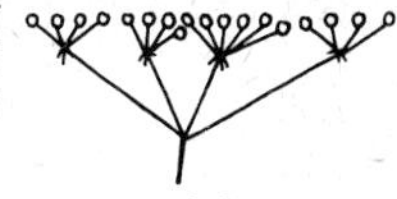

Umbels

Variegated marked with different patches of colour; dappled.

Versatile when the anther is so connected to the filament that it swings freely, as if balanced on a pivot.

Whorl a ring of leaves or flowers around a stem.

Zone a band or girdle of colour.

SOWING, PLANTING AND FLOWERING CHART

(*pages 31–34*)

(A) Annuals or grown as annuals
(B) Biennials or grown as biennials
(P) Perennials
c Best kinds for cutting
s Sow seed
s* Sow seed in warm greenhouse
– Planting out or main planting period
f Main flowering period

Note: some genera may include both annual and perennial species, e.g. *Helianthus*, *Scabiosa*. Check Descriptions section for more detailed information.

	J	F	M	A	M	J	J	A	S	O	N	D
Achillea (P) c			–			f	f	f	f	f		
Aconitum (P)			–			f	f	f	f			
Adonis (A)				s			f	f	f			
Agapanthus (P)				–			f	f	f			
Ageratum (A)			s*			–	f	f	f			
Alstroemeria (P) c						f	f	f	–			
Althaea (B)						s		f	f			
Alyssum (A)			s*			–	f	f	f			
Amaranthus (A)			s*			–	f	f	f			
Amaryllis (P)							–	f	f			
Anchusa (P)			–			f	f					
Anemone (P) c		f	f	f					–			
Anthemis (P) c			–			f	f	f		–		
Antirrhinum (A)			s*			–	f	f	f			
Aquilegia (P) c					f	f				–		
Arabis (P)			–	f	f	f						
Armeria (P)			–			f						
Aster (P) c			–					f	f	f		
Astilbe (P) c			–				f	f		–		
Aubreta (P)			–	f	f	f						
Begonia (A)			s*			–	f	f	f			
Bellis (B)			f	f	f	s			–			
Bergenia (P)			f	f						–		
Calendula (A) c				s			f	f	f			
Callistephus (A) c				s				f	f	f		
Campanula (B)					s	f			–			
Campanula (P)			–			f	f	f		–		
Centaurea (A) c				s			f	f	f			
Cheiranthus (B)			f	f	s				–			
Chionodoxa (P)		f							–			
Chrysanthemum (A)				s			f	f	f	f		
Chrysanthemum (P) c			–	–				f	f	f		
Clarkia c				s			f	f	f			
Clematis (P)				–		f	f	f	f			
Colchicum (P)								–	f	f		
Collinsia (A)				s			f	f	f			
Convallaria (P) c					f	f				–		
Convolvulus (A)				s			f	f	f			

	J	F	M	A	M	J	J	A	S	O	N	D
Coreopsis (A) c				s			f	f				
Coreopsis (P) c			–				f	f		–		
Cosmos (A)				s			f	f				
Crocosmia (P)				–				f	f			
Crocus (P)		f	f						–	f	f	
Cyclamen (P)	f	f					–	f	f			
Dahlia (A) c						–		f	f	f		
Delphinium (A) c				s			f	f				
Delphinium (P) c			–			f	f					
Dianthus (P) c			–			f	f					
Dicentra (P)				f	f	f				–		
Dictamnus (P)			–			f	f			–		
Digitalis (B)					s	f			–			
Doronicum (P) c			f	f						–		
Echinops (P) c			–				f	f				
Eranthis (P)	f	f	f						–			
Eremurus (P)					f	f	f					
Erigeron (P) c			–			f	f	f	f	–		
Eryngium (P) c			–				f	f	f			
Eschscholzia (A)				s		f	f	f	f	f		
Filipendula (P)			–			f	f	f		–		
Fuchsia (A)						–	f	f				
Gaillardia (P) c			–			f	f	f	f	–		
Galanthus (P) c	f	f	f	–								
Geranium (P)			–			f	f	f		–		
Geum (P) c			–			f	f			–		
Gladiolus (P) c			–	–		f	f	f				
Godetia (A) c				s			f	f	f			
Gypsophila (P) c			–			f	f	f				
Helenium (P) c			–				f	f	f	–		
Helianthus (A)				s				f	f			
Helichrysum (A) c				s			f	f	f			
Heliopsis (P) c			–				f	f	f	–		
Heliotropium (A)						–	f	f	f			
Helleborus (P) c		f	f							–		
Hemerocallis (P) c			–			f	f	f	f	–		
Heuchera (P)			–		f	f				–		
Hyacinthus (P)				f					–			

	J	F	M	A	M	J	J	A	S	O	N	D
Iberis (A)				s			f	f	f			
Impatiens (A)				s			f	f	f			
Incarvillea (P)			–		f	f						
Ipomoea (A)			s*			–	f	f	f			
Iris (P) c					f	f	–					
Kentranthus (P)			–			f	f	f	f	–		
Kniphofia (P)			–				f	f	f	f		
Lathyrus (A) c		s*		–		f	f					
Lavatera (A)				s			f	f	f			
Lilium auratum (P)							f	f	–			
Lilium x *hollandicum* (P)						f	f	–				
Lilium martagon (P)						f	f	–				
Limonium (P) c			–				f	f	f	–		
Linaria (A)				s			f	f	f			
Linum (P)			–				f	f	f	–		
Lobelia (A)			s*			–	f	f	f			
Lunaria (B) c				f	f	s			–			
Lupinus (P)			–		f	f						
Lychnis (A)				s			f	f	f			
Lysimachia (P)			–			f	f	f	f	–		
Malva (P)			–				f	f	f	–		
Matthiola (B) c					f	f	s		–			
Meconopsis (P)			s*		f	f	f					
Mesembryanthemum (A)			s*			–	f	f	f			
Mimulus (A)			s*			–	f	f	f			
Mirabilis (A)			s*			–	f	f	f			
Muscari (P)			f	f					–			
Myosotis (B)			f	f		s			–			
Narcissus (P) c			f	f	f			–				
Nemesia (A)			s*			–	f	f	f			
Nepeta (P)			–		f	f	f	f	f	–		
Nicotiana (A)			s*			–	f	f	f	f		
Nigella (A) c				s			f	f	f			
Oenothera (P)			–			f	f	f		–		
Paeonia (P) c						f				–		
Papaver (A)				s		f	f	f				
Papaver (P)			–			f						

	J	F	M	A	M	J	J	A	S	O	N	D
Pelargonium (A)						–	f	f	f			
Penstemon (A) c						–	f	f	f			
Petunia (A)			s*			–	f	f	f			
Phacelia (A)				s			f	f	f			
Phlox (P)			–				f	f		–		
Physalis (P) c			–				f			–		
Polemonium (P)			–			f	f	f	f	–		
Polygonatum (P)			–		f	f				–		
Portulaca (A)				s			f	f	f			
Potentilla (P)			–			f	f	f	f			
Primula (P)			s*	f	f	f	f					
Pyrethrum (P) c			–		f	f				–		
Ranunculus (P)			–		f	f				–		
Reseda (A) c				s			f	f				
Romneya (P)			–			f	f	f	f			
Rudbeckia (A) c			s*			–		f	f	f		
Salpiglossis (A) c			s*			–	f	f	f			
Salvia (A)			s*			–	f	f	f			
Saponaria (P)			–				f	f	f	–		
Scabiosa (P) c			–			f	f	f	f	–		
Scilla (P)		f	f		f	f			–			
Sedum (P)			–					f	f	–		
Solidago (P) c			–				f	f	f	–		
Sternbergia (P)								–	f	f		
Tagetes (A)			s*			–	f	f	f	f		
Thalictrum (P)			–		f	f	f			–		
Thymus (P)			–			f	f	f	f	–		
Tigridia (P)				–			f	f	f			
Tradescantia (P)			–			f	f			–		
Trollius (P)			–		f	f				–		
Tropaeolum (A)				s			f	f	f	f		
Tulipa (P) c				f	f					–		
Verbascum (B)					s	f	f		–			
Verbena (A)			s*			–	f	f	f	f		
Veronica (P)			–		f	f	f	f	f	–		
Viola (B)			f	f	s				–			
Zinnia (A)			s*			–	f	f	f			

DESCRIPTION OF SPECIES

In the following pages the letters **A, B** and **P,** indicate that the subject is (or is best treated as) annual, biennial or perennial.

Family COMPOSITAE *Achillea* species

A genus of about a hundred perennial species, widespread through the Northern Hemisphere, varying in height from a few centimetres to 150 to 180 cm and with flowers usually in flat corymbs. *A. millefolium*, height 60 to 90 cm, is a white-flowered British species; good garden forms are 'Cerise Queen' and 'Fire King'. From *A. filipendula* (*A. eupatorium*), reaching 120 cm, flowers mustard yellow, have arisen as garden forms or as hybrids (with other species), 'Coronation Gold', small flower-heads, golden yellow; 'Gold Plate', deep golden yellow; 'Moonshine', silvery leaves, bright canary yellow, 60 cm; 'Clypeolata', bright yellow, 45 cm; 'Taygetea', light yellow with grey foliage, 60 cm. *A. ptarmica*, Europe including Britain, has broad heads of white flowers, height 60 cm. 'Perry's White' is a double-flowered form. 'The Pearl' also double-flowered, white, has slightly larger flowers. Both are excellent for cutting. Achilleas grow well in any well-drained soil in sunny situations.

Propagation is by division. The various species can be raised from seed. **Flowering** from June to September.

Monkshood **P**

Family RANUNCULACEAE *Aconitum* species

Ornamental herbaceous perennials of tall stature native to Europe, temperate Asia and North America. The roots and foliage of certain species yield drugs valued for medicinal purposes; all are reputed to be poisonous.

For herbaceous borders certain species only are important. *A. napellus* is the best known; the blue flowers are borne in racemes and have the upper sepal formed into a hood or helmet. *A. vulparia* is 90 to 180 cm high, has yellow flowers with a longer and narrower head; *A. carmichaelii* (syn. *A. fischeri*) attains a height of 30 cm, bearing racemes of deep purple-blue hooded flowers. Hybrids of particular garden value include *A. × bicolor*, A. 'Blue Sceptre', *A. 'Arendsii'* and A. 'Bressingham Spire'. At the back of herbaceous borders the Aconitums are effective. They are easily cultivated in any moderately rich, moist, well-drained garden soil. In sun or semi-shade.

Propagation is by seeds sown as soon as ripe or by division in early autumn or spring. **Flowering** is June and July for *A. napellus*, June to September for *A. vulparia*, and September for *A. carmichaelii.*

Family RANUNCULACEAE *Adonis* species

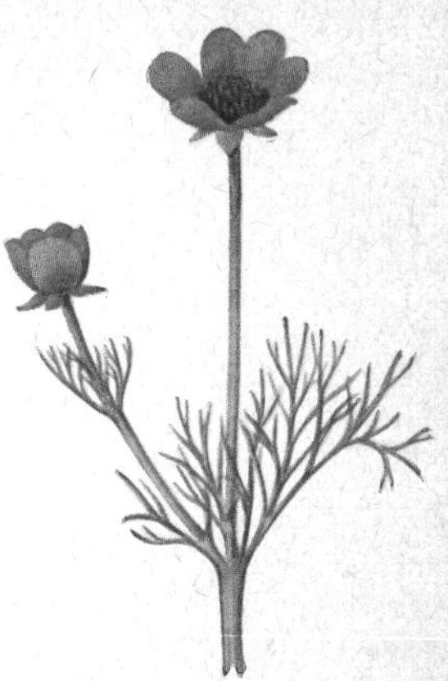

The annual species are brightly coloured, of Syrian and European origin and hardy in Britain. The leaves are finely cut and fern-like; flowers vary in colour according to the species. *A. aestivalis* (pheasant's eye), has almost blood-red flowers, 2½ cm across, with dark centres, on 30-cm stems. *A. autumnalis* (*A. annua*) has scarlet flowers on 30-cm stems. The Syrian, *A. aleppica*, has brilliant scarlet flowers, 5 cm across, freely produced; it reaches a height of 30 cm.

Among the most brilliant of annuals, the Adonis with its scarlet flowers makes a bright splash of colour in the annual border. Sow seed in autumn or spring where the plants are to flower, and thin to 10 cm apart in spring.

A. amurensis, flowering in March and April, is a yellow-flowered perennial species growing to about 45 cm high. There are white, pink and orange forms, also a double-flowered form. A native of Manchuria, it dies down in late summer. *A. vernalis*, of European origin, also yellow-flowered, grows to 30 cm in height and flowers in March.

Propagation of the perennial species is from seed or by division in early spring; the various other forms by division. **Flowering** early summer for *A. aestivalis*, late summer for the other two annual species.

Family LILIACEAEA *Agapanthus africanus*

Also known as *A. umbellatus and* lily-of-the Nile, although it is a native of S. Africa. The foliage is abundant, long, thick and narrow, rising from 60 to 90 cm and bright green. The flowers, about 2½ cm across, are borne in large umbels on leafless stems to a height of 90 cm or more, as many as twenty or thirty flowers composing a single umbel. The colour is pale to deep blue. There is also a white flowered form.

A. africanus and its forms are hardy out of doors only in the milder parts of Britain, particularly in the west and south-west. The Headbourne Hybrids strain is probably the hardiest of the agapanthus, flower colour ranging from pale blue to deep violet-blue.

The position must be in full sun, and a rich, deep, well-drained soil is necessary to grow these plants satisfactorily. Spring frost protection with loose litter is advisable in colder areas. They make excellent tub plants.

Propagation is by division in spring or by seed sown in the autumn. **Flowering** July and August.

Family COMPOSITAE *Ageratum houstonianum*

Noted for its blue flowers, this half-hardy annual of Mexican origin is very popular in the annual flower border. Known also as *A. mexicanum*. The leaves are small, ovate and toothed; the flowers of blue or white are borne in fluffy heads with great freedom. The species is represented by its garden varieties; there are dwarf forms, not exceeding 15 cm high, such as 'Blue Chip' and 'Little Blue Star', both with blue flowers; 'Blue Mink' is popular, having a taller stature with freely produced flowers of powder blue; 'Blue Ball' and 'Blue Cap' have deep blue flowers and neat compact habits. 'Blue Blazer', bluish-mauve, and 'Summer Snow' white, make an attractive low-growing combination, together growing to little more than 10 cm in height. 'Fairy Pink', rose-pink, and 'Violet Cloud', violet-blue, both reach 15 cm.

The seed should be sown in boxes under glass in March, the seedlings pricked off and subsequently hardened off for planting out in June, 15 to 20 cm apart, when the risk of frost is past.

Propagation is from seed. **Flowering** from late June until the end of September.

Family AMARYLLIDACEAE *Alstroemeria* species

A race of colourful lily-like perennials, natives of tropical and sub-tropical South America of which a number of species are hardy in Britain. Although sun lovers, the more robust species grow well under semi-shaded conditions.

A. aurantiaca has given rise to a number of improved garden forms all producing bright orange flowers borne on 60- to 90-cm stems; 'Lutea' has yellow flowers, 'Dover Orange' orange-red. *A. pulchella* (syn. *psittacina*) has tubular flowers pale red below, green above. *A. ligtu* var. *angustifolia* and its hybrids, known collectively as '*Ligtu* Hybrids', produce large heads of flowers from cream to rich peach, apricot, salmon and rose. *A. haemantha* has smaller flowers of deep red.

Alstroemerias are easily grown in deep sandy soil in sun or semi-shade and the roots should be planted 15 to 20 cm below the surface. They require three years in which to become established. Plant in October or early spring.

Propagation is by division of the fleshy-rooted crowns, or by seed sown in gentle warmth in early spring. **Flowering** in July.

Hollyhock

Family Malvaceae *Althaea rosea*

For many years a feature of cottage gardens in Britain, originally introduced from China, where it is a native. Although perennial, it is generally treated as a biennial. There are both single- and double-flowered forms, many flowers, 10 to 15 cm in diameter, being borne on substantial stems that will attain a height of more than 2 metres. The colours range from white and yellow to shades of pink to scarlet, crimson and purple. 'Silver Puffs' is a dwarf type, 60 cm in height, silvery-pink. Planted in groups at the back of the border, the hollyhock lends itself to bold effect, especially if planted against a background of dark green. The foliage is large and rounded and is produced beneath the flower-spike; it is often subject to hollyhock rust disease (for control see notes on diseases in Introduction). For successful cultivation a deep loamy soil, good drainage and a sunny position are essential.

Propagation. Best treated as a biennial by sowing seed in June to produce plants that will flower the following year, but there are annual strains that can be sown under glass in March to flower the same year. **Flowering** in August and September.

Sweet Alyssum **A P**

Family CRUCIFERAE *Alyssum* species

A native of southern Europe *A. maritimum* (botanically correct name *Lobularia maritimum*) is a perennial, but is best treated as an annual. The plant, when full grown, will not exceed 30 cm in height with a spread of 30 cm across. The foliage is minute and almost entirely hidden by the freely produced white flowers; it owes its popular name to its fragrance. The forms of garden origin enjoy considerable popularity as edging plants for summer bedding schemes, growing from 7 to 30 cm in height. There are numerous varieties in shades of blue, pink and white, e.g., 'Little Dorritt', 'Rosy O'Day', 'Violet Queen'. The seed should be sown in March under glass, the seedlings pricked off and planted out where they are to flower when the risk of frost has passed; or outdoors in early May.

Propagation is from seed. **Flowering** from midsummer until frost.

A. saxatile (syn. *Aurinia saxatilis*), the yellow alyssum, is a perennial from Eastern Europe. Shrubby at the base, the twisting flower stems attain a height of about 30 cm. 'Citrinum', 'Compactum' and 'Plenum' are good forms. The flowering period is April to June. *A. argenteum*, up to 45 cm, flowers from June to August.

Love-lies-bleeding

Family AMARANTHACEAE *Amaranthus* species

A genus comprising about fifty half-hardy annuals of coarse growth and native to mild and tropical countries in many parts of the world. The foliage is large, oval and pointed, and the flowers are small and numerous, forming into a drooping tassel-like raceme. The familiar love-lies-bleeding is *A. caudatus*: 60 to 90 cm, it hails from the tropics and has drooping reddish stems bearing purple flowers; its form 'Atropurpureus' is of a slightly deeper and richer tone; 'Viridis' is a white-flowered form similar in habit to the foregoing. There are several good colour forms available under varietal names. Known as Joseph's coat, *A. tricolor* (possibly a form of *A. gangeticus*) from India, has red, green and yellow foliage. There are several forms with considerable variation in foliage colouring, adding combinations of bronze, gold, orange and scarlet. The drooping purple flowers are of little value and are best removed.

Seed may be sown under glass with artificial heat in March, pricked off into boxes or pots when 2·5 cm high and planted out of doors in June.

Propagation is from seed. **Flowering** from midsummer onwards.

Belladonna Lily

Family AMARYLLIDACEAE *Amaryllis belladonna*

Introduced to our gardens from Cape Colony in 1712. The bulbs produce deep green leaves, strap-shaped and up to 45 cm long. The flower-stems reach about the same height and bear from five to twelve large funnel-shaped flowers, not unlike some species of lilies; these are soft rose in colour and delightfully perfumed.

There are various forms of the belladonna lily: var. *kewensis*, var. *elata*, var. *rubra*. A number of improved hybrids, such as 'Barberton', 'Cape Town', and 'Johannesburg' have been introduced in recent years. Plant just below ground level in autumn in a well-drained soil enriched with leaf-mould or granulated peat. A sheltered border at the foot of a south-facing wall is an ideal position. Where the winter is severe a protective litter of bracken should be placed over the position where the bulbs are planted. Once the bulbs are established it is not wise to disturb them for at least five years, then, if crowded, they may be transplanted if desired as soon as the foliage ripens.

Propagation is by offsets removed when the bulbs have been lifted and ripened. **Flowering** in August and September.

Family Boraginaceae *Anchusa* species

One of the loveliest of all blue-flowered perennials and a native of the Mediterranean region containing species of both tall and dwarf stature and a number of garden origin.

A. azurea (syn. *A. italica*) reaches a height of from 90 cm to 1·5 metres; it is best known by its garden forms, e,g., 'Dropmore', 'Pride of Dover', 'Opal', 'Loddon Royalist', the most outstanding of the taller forms, and 'Morning Glory', tallest of all. The flowers are round, less than 2·5 cm across, of varying shades of blue. *A. caespitosa*, a native of Crete, is 30 to 45 cm high and produces masses of brilliant blue flowers, white centred. The coarseness of the roots of the *azurea* forms makes a well-drained soil imperative, a wet soil causing decay. *A. caespitosa* also prefers well-drained soils and all are sun lovers.

Propagate from root cuttings, in the early spring, *A. caespitosa* from crown cuttings. **Flowering** from spring to early summer.

A. capensis is a biennial, usually grown as an annual, introduced from South Africa, height about 45 cm, with bright blue flowers, it is hardy and can be sown in the open border in April.

Family RANUNCULACEAE *Anemone* species

A large genus chiefly found in north temperate and mountainous regions. Apart from many dwarf species that are eminently suitable for rock gardens, there are others that have particular value in herbaceous borders. *A. coronaria* is noteworthy as having given rise to the famous St. Brigid strain with a colour range that varies from white to shades of pink, crimson, purple and almost blue. The flowers reach a height of 30 cm when well grown in a rich soil. *A.* × *hybrida* (syn. *A. elegans.*, *A. japonica*) is a name covering the group of hybrids known as Japanese anemones, with names such as 'Lorelei', 'Margarita', 'Max Vogel', etc. They are of herbaceous habit with elegantly cut foliage and branching stems, bearing large flowers, 7·5 cm across, of white, pink or purple in late summer.

A rich sandy loam, into which leaf-mould has been introduced, is necessary for the best results.

Propagation is by seed for the St. Brigid Anemones, and by division or root cuttings for *A.* × *hybrida*. **Flowering** throughout the greater part of the year for the St. Brigid varieties, and in late summer for *A.* × *hybrida*.

Family Compositae *Anthemis* species

Anthemis tinctoria is a perennial species of a genus that inhabits the temperate regions of the Old World. Many flower-heads are borne on branching stems that attain a height of 60 to 90 cm, the yellow rays spreading from a central yellow disc. Also known as the yellow marguerite.

The species is not now widely grown, having been superseded by the varieties of garden origin that have originated from it with flowers up to 7·5 cm across, notably 'Perry's Variety', golden yellow, 'Grallagh Gold', an even deeper yellow, 'Wargrave Variety', cream and 'E. C. Buxton', lemon-yellow. *A. sancti-johannis* with orange-yellow flowers is a closely related smaller, tufted species which hybridizes with *A. tinctoria* in gardens. The foliage is finely cut and aromatic when crushed. Very hardy and becoming established over a period of many years. Much valued as a decorative cut flower. Grows in full sun in any good porous soil. *A. nobilis*, easily raised from seed, is used for chamomile lawns, the non-flowering form 'Treneague' being best for this purpose.

Propagation is by seed, division of established clumps and by cuttings in early spring. **Flowering** from June until late summer.

Snapdragon

Family SCROPHULARIACEAE *Antirrhinum majus*

A native of the Mediterranean region and a firm favourite in British gardens, where it is usually grown as a half-hardy annual although it is, in fact, a perennial. The flowers are borne in spikes, are tubular in shape, with spreading lobes of irregular formation. The many varieties of garden origin show a considerable colour range which may extend from white, cream and shades of yellow to pink, terra-cotta, scarlet and crimson tones. There are also forms with double flowers and with ruffled blooms, and an increasing number of rust-resistant varieties. There is a considerable variation in height within the three basic groups: dwarf, cushion-like 10 to 20 cm; intermediate, 45 to 60 cm; tall, 90 cm. 'Floral Cluster', 'Floral Carpet' and 'Little Gem' are amongst the best of the dwarf multi-coloured strains.

Snapdragons will grow well in any ordinary soil in a sunny position. Apart from their value in the border the dwarf and medium varieties can be grown as ornamental pot plants.

Propagation may be by seed, under glass in January to March, to flower from June to October, or in the open in late summer or early autumn to bloom the following spring, or by cuttings.

Flowering from spring until well into autumn.

Columbine

Family RANUNCULACEAE *Aquilegia* species

An old garden favourite, *A. vulgaris*, the common columbine, is native to Europe. The newer forms originated from the fusion of various species that are native to North America and parts of Asia, notably Siberia and Japan. The plants form compact clumps with foliage of fern-like aspect and stems of varying height, carrying branching stems bearing singly many flowers, 5 cm or more across, and noteworthy on account of their long spurs. Long-spurred hybrids (*A.* × *hybrida*) are the most usually planted, originating from the red and yellow species *A. formosa*, *A. canadensis* and *A. skinneri* as well as the soft golden yellow *A. chrysantha* and the blue *A. caerulea*. 'Crimson Star', is a hybrid with red and white flowers, reaching about 60 cm in height. 'Dragonfly' is a brightly coloured strain. 'Snow Queen' is pure white, 45 cm high. There are several alpine species such as *A. alpina*, about 30 cm in height, and *A. bertolonii*, about 15 cm.

At the front of the border the columbine should be massed for effect, and so long as the soil is reasonably moist and fertile it will give a good account of itself. Partial shade is preferred.

Propagation is by seed sown as soon as ripe to produce plants that will flower in the following year. **Flowering** in May and June.

Family CRUCIFERAE *Arabis albida*

The genus comprises many species native to Europe and America of which a number are alpine. The flowers are small and borne on stems, a few centimetres high, in terminal racemes over a considerable period of time. The plants are leafy and of tuft-like growth, but inclined to become straggling if not cut back annually.

A. albida (syn. *A. caucasica*), the white arabis, provides masses of small white flowers of single form, but is not often grown today, having given place to the free-flowering double white form 'Flore Pleno'. The fragrant flowers are useful to form carpets at the front of herbaceous borders. There is also a pink flowered form 'Rosabella', a red-flowered form, 'Coccinea', and a slow-growing variegated-leaved form, but their place is rather in the rock garden than the perennial border. One of the easiest plants to cultivate, the arabis will grow in any reasonably well-drained soil in either partial shade or in full sun.

Propagation is by division, seed or cuttings. **Flowering** from March to May.

Family PLUMBAGINACEAE *Armeria maritima*

Also known as the sea pink, the genus has its various species in Europe, western Asia, North Africa and North America. The species most used in gardens is *A. maritima*, the common thrift, a native of the coastal regions of North America and Europe. The tightly clustered heads of small flowers vary from white to pale pink in the native state, but in rich pink and reddish purple tones in varieties of garden origin. 'Bloodstone' is an excellent red-flowered form. 'Bee's Ruby' is a hybrid of uncertain origin with stems fully 30 cm high and bearing large heads of ruby-red flowers; it is, in every way, a giant form of thrift and most useful for planting in the front of the border. *A. corsica* (possibly a form of *A. maritima*) 12 to 23 cm, has brick-red flowers. *A. caespitosa*, a native of Spain, forming dense 5- to 7-cm cushions with pale lilac flowers, is more usually associated with the rock garden. 'Bevan's Variety' is a particularly distinct form.

In cultivation armerias demand full sun and ample drainage, it being wise, except in the most porous soils, to incorporate plenty of coarse grit into the soil around the roots.

Propagate by seed or division of the roots in early spring. **Flowering** from late May until early July.

Michaelmas Daisy

Family COMPOSITAE *Aster* species

The Michaelmas daisies comprise hybrids and forms of several different species of *Aster*: *A. amellus*, from Italy, *A. novae-angliae* and *A. novi-belgii*, both of North American origin, all September-flowering and varying from 60 cm (in the case of *A. amellus* and forms) to 1·5 metres in height. The flowers vary from less than 2·5 cm to 7·5 cm across, colour from white to pink, blue, purple and violet. *A. cordifolius* forms are tall, bearing masses of small flowers of various shades. *A.* × *frikartii* has large violet-blue flowers, amongst the best of the genus.

Other asters: *A. acris*, from Southern Europe, about 90 cm tall, has mauve, golden-centred flowers; *A. yunnanensis*, 22 to 30 cm high, bears solitary heliotrope-blue flowers in early summer; *A. ericoides* forms bear a profusion of small, star-like flowers in September and October. There are also a number of dwarf hybrids.

Asters grow well in full sun and in almost all soils.

Propagation is by division in autumn or spring. **Flowering** from June to October.

Family SAXIFRAGACECAE *Astilbe* species

Comprises about fourteen species inhabiting moist places in eastern Asia and eastern North America. The plants are mostly of tall habit, with elegant fern-like foliage and small flowers, varying from white to shades of pink, salmon, purple and red, borne in dense spikes that form feathery panicles.

The present race of garden varieties is believed to have originated from crosses between *A. astilboides* and *A. thunbergii* (with probably the occasional use of *A. rutilans*, *A. carmina*, *A. japonica* and *A. davidii*). These various hybrids are usually grouped under *A.* × *arendsii*, after the German hybridist, Arends. Among the many named hybrids are 'Irrlich', white, 'Fanal', red, 'Intermezzo', salmon-pink, 'Ostrich Plume', clear pink, 'Red Sentinel', brick-red. For the middle portion of the border and on the banks of ponds or streams or where there is partial shade but the soil is never really dry, the astilbes are to be seen under the most suitable conditions. *A. simplicifolia*, *A.* × *crispa* and *A.* × *humilis* are attractive miniatures valuable for rock gardens.

Propagate by division or seeds. **Flowering** from July until late August.

Family CRUCIFERAE *Aubrieta deltoidea*

Aubrietas are a colourful and almost evergreen race of trailing plants of the eastern Mediterranean region from Sicily to Persia. The best-known species is *A. deltoidea.* The many garden forms are of mixed origin although most are probably derived from *A. deltoidea.* They have small spoon-shaped foliage, toothed and greyish green in colour, with single flowers, about 1 cm across, varying in shade, among garden forms, from pale pink to lavender, purple and crimson. 'Bressingham Pink', deep pink, 'Dr. Mules', violet-blue, and 'Magician', bright purple, are deservedly popular. There are also double forms of garden origin and a form with variegated foliage.

The aubrietas are useful for the front of the herbaceous border, their trailing growths breaking the line of formal edging and providing profuse bloom in season. They are excellent rock garden plants. It is wise to cut back after flowering in order to maintain a tidy habit of growth. They can be grown successfully in any well-drained soil in full sun. Usually planted from pots in early March.

Propagate from cuttings for preference, by division or by seed. **Flowering** in spring and early summer.

Family BEGONIACEAE *Begonia × tuberhybrida*

A name given to the tuberous begonias of garden origin derived from such species as *B. boliviensis*, *B. clarkei*, *B. davisii*, *B. pearcei*, *B. rosiflora*, *B. veitchii* and others from the tropics that are used for outdoor planting in summer although best suited for greenhouse culture owing to their flowers becoming weighed down by rain and spoiled. They exhibit a very wide range of colours from white and shades of yellow to pink, salmon, orange, scarlet, crimson. The Multiflora group of continental origin, e.g. 'Flamboyant', 'Helen Harmes', are dwarf-growing and excellent for bedding out. The tubers may be potted in March in a cool greenhouse and are planted out of doors in early June. *B. semperflorens*, from Brazil, a tender perennial grown as a half-hardy annual, is very popular in its many varieties. Leaves are roundish, bright green to deep bronze. Flowers from white, through many shades of pink to deep scarlet. Height from 15 to 45 cm. The soil should have been well enriched by the previous incorporation of old manure and the position should enjoy full sun. Perfect drainage is essential.

Propagation is by means of seed or cuttings. **Flowering** in summer.

Family COMPOSITAE *Bellis perennis*

A native of Europe and the Mediterranean region. The present garden forms with double flowers originated from the wild daisy of our meadows. The leaves are strap-shaped, widening towards the end, and form a basal tuft. The flowers are freely borne on 15-cm stems and attain a diameter up to 5 cm, varying in colour from white to shades of pink and red. An old favourite is the hen and chickens daisy, so called from its curious habit of producing secondary and smaller flowers from the scales when the main flowers are fully developed. This old-fashioned plant is seen to best effect when massed in generous batches of one colour. 'Rob Roy' is a brilliant red form. 'Dresden China' is soft pink. There are also several good strains of mixed colours. 'Monstrosa' is a giant-flowered form. Although perennial they are usually grown as biennials and are of the simplest culture, requiring a good normal garden soil, well drained and exposed to the sun or in partial shade. Planting may be carried out in late summer or in February or March.

Propagation is effected by division of selected forms in spring or from seed sown in May. **Flowering** in spring and early summer.

Family SAXIFRAGACEAE *Bergenia* species

Bergenia cordifolia is from a large genus comprising mostly plants for the rock garden.

The plant is from Siberia and has large dark, glossy green foliage, heart-shaped and produced in profusion. The flowers are 20 mm or more across, of a variable shade of rose pink and borne on thick, fleshy stems from 30 cm to 45 cm high, and barely rising above the foliage. Other species which may be encountered include *B. crassifolia*, with red flowers and a rather woody rootstock, and *B. purpurascens* with purple flowers and less than 30 cm in height. There are a number of hybrids and forms of garden origin, among the best being 'Silberlicht', flowers white, suffused pink, 'Evening Glow', rosy-red, 'Ballawley Hybrid', clear rose-pink, 'Margery Fish', pink.

Bergenias will grow in any position—and in any soil—but, being early flowering, one that faces due south or is protected somewhat from wintry weather is preferable.

Propagate by division of the root or from seed. **Flowering** is in early spring.

Pot Marigold **A**

Family Compositae 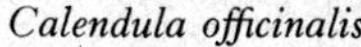 *Calendula officinalis*

A native of southern Europe and an old garden favourite. The common name owes its origin to old-time use of the flower petals for flavouring. The leaves are hairy, coarse and oblongish. The thick branching stems grow up to 60 cm, with flowers, 10 cm across, of flat white-yellow to deep orange rays that tend to close at night. The species owes its present great popularity to the number of varieties of garden origin, with fully double flowers such as 'Lemon Queen', 'Orange King Improved', and 'Radio' with fluted petals, that vary in tones of apricot, lemon, sulphur and golden-yellow. Other good strains are 'Geisha Girl', reddish-orange blooms with incurved petals, 'Orange Coronet', golden-orange, a compact 30 cm and 'Art Shades', shades of cream and orange with brown centres.

One of the easiest of plants to grow, the seed may be sown in March or April, where the plants are to bloom. As germination is free, seed should be sown sparingly, thinning seedlings 30 cm apart. The position may be in full sun or partial shade. Much valued as a cut flower, and may be grown for a long season if protected by cloches in early spring and late autumn to guard against frosts.

Propagate from seed. **Flowering** from February to early December.

Family Compositae *Callistephus chinensis*

One of the most popular of all annuals, being native to China and Japan. The type has deeply lobed, hairy, ovate leaves; branching stems of 30 to 75 cm, and flowers with ray petals surrounding a yellow central disc. The many garden forms have flowers which range from white to shades of violet, purple, blue, rose and yellow, including bicolours, often 12 cm across. Some of the most outstanding garden forms are 'Ostrich Plumes', with feathery petals; 'Paeony Flowered', with incurved flowers; 'Comet', double flowers with loosely arranged rays or petals; 'Anemone Flowered', with flat florets around a quilled centre; 'Chrysanthemum Flowered', with large fully double flowers; 'Pompon', with small fully double flowers, 'Lilliput', a dwarf group. Plants are usually raised from seed sown early in the year in heat, 55° to 65° F., pricked off into boxes of compost, and finally planted out in May. May also be sown in cold frame in early April, or out of doors in mid-April.

Propagate from seed. **Flowering** from late June until the end of September.

Family CAMPANULACEAE *Campanula* species (biennial)

A native of southern Europe, *C. medium* is the most popular of the biennial campanulas reaching 60 to 90 cm. The flowers of the type are violet-blue, borne two or more together in long open racemes. *C. m.* '*Calycanthema*' is a hose in hose type. There are shades of violet-blue, pink and white in both forms and a neat dwarf strain 'Bells of Holland', reaching about 38 cm in height. From Greece we have *C. ramosissima* (syn. *C. loreyi*), reaching up to 22 cm high, with saucer-shaped flowers, 2·5 cm across, of parma-violet changing to white at the base. Reaching a height of 45 cm, *C. thyrsoidea*, from the European Alps, is a somewhat hairy plant; the flowers are straw-yellow, of tubular form, borne in a close spike, *C. pyramidalis* has spikes up to 182 cm high, densely covered with blue or white open bells. Perennial, it is usually grown as a biennial. There are also a number of alpine forms. Of those named, only *C. ramosissima* is annual. The seed of the biennial types is sown in May or June, the seedlings pricked off into nursery beds for transplanting in the autumn.

Propagation is from seed. **Flowering** in summer.

Family CAMPANULACEAE *Campanula* species (perennial)

A large genus of perennials, annuals and biennials, widely spread over nearly all the northern hemisphere. The greater number are suitable for rock gardens, being of dwarf habit. Those of sufficient vigour and possessing a habit suiting them to herbaceous borders comprise *C. persicifolia,* perhaps the best of the border species rising to 90 cm and bearing large bell-shaped flowers of lavender or white in double or single form; named forms include 'Talham Beauty', rich blue, and 'Snowdrift', white; *C. lactiflora* with branching stems up to 120 cm, bearing panicles of blue or white flowers; named forms 'Pouffe' and 'Pritchards Variety'; *C. latifolia,* up to 150 cm, with racemes of larger, violet-purple flowers, and its darker form 'Brantwood'; *C. glomerata* and its form 'Dahurica' with clustered heads of deep purple flowers on 45-cm stems.

Easily cultivated in a well-drained soil.

Propagate by division of the roots in early spring or from seed. **Flowering** in June and July.

Cornflower **A P**

Family Compositae *Centaurea* species

The most popular of the annual cornflowers is *C. cyanus* a native of Britain and Europe and one of the most attractive of hardy annuals. The varieties of garden origin contain a wide range of colours, but the most pleasing are those of blue and pink shades. There are also double-flowered forms and dwarf strains. One of the most attractive annual species, particularly as a cut flower, is *C. moschata*, from Persia, commonly known as sweet sultan.

Easily grown from seed sown in March to April out of doors where the plants are to flower, being thinned to 10 to 15 cm apart. A position in full sun is necessary, and well-drained moderately rich soil.

Propagation is from seed. **Flowering** from midsummer onwards.

Most of the perennial cornflowers, such as *C. montana* and *C. ruthenica*, are from the Caucasus or Eastern Europe. They are not as charming as the annuals, but *C. dealbata* 'John Coutts' 60 cm in height, clear pink, is worthy of a place in the border. *C. macrocephala*, 150 cm in height, with yellow flowers, is also useful for the back of the border.

Family Cruciferae *Cheiranthus cheiri*

A native of the sea cliffs, quarries and old walls of southern Europe, hence its common name. One of the best loved of plants, and naturalized in parts of Britain, the wallflower is really a perennial, but usually treated as a biennial. The plant is of bushy erect habit, 30 to 60 cm high, with fragrant flowers, about 2·5 cm across, yellow or brownish-yellow in the type, but varying from off-white to pink, terra-cotta, orange, scarlet and crimson in varieties of garden origin. There are also dwarf strains growing to no more than 22 cm in height. 'Harpur Crewe', with golden yellow, double flowers, is a good, long-established form. There are many other forms and strains. *C. allionii*, a native of North America, is called the Siberian wallflower. It has been suggested that it may be an *Erysimum* hybrid. Reaching a height of 22 cm, its heads of bright orange flowers in late spring are welcome successors to the true wallflower. A closely related, pretty mauve-flowered plant is *Erysimum linifolium*, sometimes called *C. linifolium*.

Seed should be sown in the open in late May or early June and the seedlings planted in their permanent positions by October.

Propagation is from seed. **Flowering** from March to May for *C. cheiri* and in May and June for *C. allionii*.

Family LILIACEAE *Chionodoxa* species

A charming bulbous genus from the high altitudes of Crete and Asia Minor. The blooms appear as the snow melts, hence their common name. The chief species is *C. luciliae*, with star-shaped six-petalled flowers, 19 mm across, of brilliant blue shading to a white centre, several flowers borne on each stem to a height of about 15 cm. There are also pink and white-flowered forms. *C. lochiae* has deep blue flowers without the white centre. *C. gigantea* has flowers twice the size of the type, while *C. sardensis* has gentian blue flowers with only a small white centre, and *C. nana* white and lilac. There is also a white form. Planted in the front of herbaceous borders, in rock gardens and naturalized in the wild garden in bold drifts, Chionodoxa give an enchanting effect early in the year.

The bulbs should be planted in early autumn, and will succeed in any well-drained soil and on grassy banks where the grass is not coarse. They may be left to establish themselves in large colonies, provided they are given a light mulch of sifted leaf-mould each autumn.

Propagation is effected by offsets and seed. **Flowering** in February.

Family COMPOSITAE *Chrysanthemum* species

The annual chrysanthemums are natives of Europe and North Africa. From Morocco comes the tricolour chrysanthemum, *C. carinatum*, with lobed leaves and 60- to 90-cm stems bearing large single flowers, 6 cm across, with ray petals of white, red, purple or yellow, with a brightly coloured ring at the central disc of purple. The European and native *C. segetum* is the corn marigold, with 30- to 60-cm high very branching stems bearing 5-cm single flowers in sprays, yellow to white in the type, but varying to canary-yellow with chocolate-coloured centres in varieties of garden origin. The garland chrysanthemum or crown daisy is *C. coronarium*, from southern Europe, up to 90 cm in height, with single yellow and white flowers set off with a cream zone at the centre. There are also double-flowered forms.

The seeds of these species may be sown in March or April where the plants are to bloom, and thinned to 30 cm apart. They will grow well in any ordinary soil, but need a sunny position.

Propagation is from seed. **Flowering** in late summer.

Perennial Chrysanthemum

Family COMPOSITAE *Chrysanthemum* species

First cultivated in ancient China circa 500 B.C. and introduced to Britain in the late 18th century, the original Chinese chrysanthemums were very limited in form and colour. However, interbreeding in Japan with native species and further breeding in Britain and elsewhere has resulted in the wide range of form and colour of modern varieties. The early-flowering section will flower in the open ground, without any protection. Raised from cuttings, under glass, after hardening off they are planted in the open in full sun, in well-manured soil, flowering from August to October. Korean Hybrids are very hardy, with small single or semi-double flowers in many colours freely produced. Height up to 75 cm. They will survive most winters out of doors.

C. maximum, the summer-flowering Shasta daisy, 90 to 120 cm tall, is a hardy perennial species. There are several varieties, e.g. 'Esther Read', 'Wirral Supreme', all white-flowered. *C. rubellum*, also perennial, has single purple-rose flowers. Named forms include 'Clara Curtis', deep pink, 'Paul Boissier', coppery-orange.

Family ONAGRACEAE *Clarkia* species

A race of four or five species of annuals native to California and among the most showy of garden flowers. *C. elegans*, the most popular species, has oval leaves with stems of a ruddy glaucous hue of 45 cm to 1·2 metres, if well grown, and many round flowers, 12 mm or less across, that are purple in the type, ranging from white to blood-red in forms of garden origin. There are also selected strains with double flowers and with irregular blotching of the blooms. *C. pulchella*, native to the west coast of America, from British Columbia to California, is a species occasionally encountered. It does not exceed 45 cm high, and has lilac-coloured flowers with the claws of the petals toothed. There is also a white-flowered form. Easily grown in any well-drained soil in full sun, the seeds being sown in April to June where the plants are to flower. Both species and their many beautiful varieties of garden origin are valuable for providing bold masses of colour in the flower garden.

Propagate from seed. **Flowering** from July to October.

Family RANUNCULACEAE

Clematis species

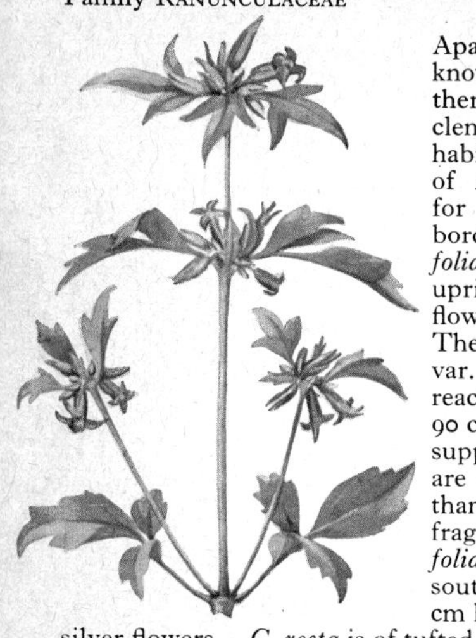

Apart from the well-known climbing forms there are several clematis of herbaceous habit, mostly natives of Asia and valuable for use in herbaceous borders. *C. heracleaefolia* is of strong and upright growth. The flowers are light blue. The best form is *C. h.* var. *davidiana*, which reaches a height of 90 cm and may need support; the flowers are of a brighter blue than the type and are fragrant. *C. integrifolia* is a native of southern Europe, 90 cm high, with blue and silver flowers. *C. recta* is of tufted habit, with pinnate leaves and many flowers 2·5 cm across, white, fragrant, and borne in branching terminal panicles to 90 cm or more in height. *C.* × *jouiniana* is a pale-blue flowered hybrid with a woody base, growing to about 120 cm in height: 'Cote d'Azur', a selected form of *C.* × *jouiniana*, has dark blue flowers.

A light, rich loam, dressed with lime, is best for clematis, and perfect drainage is essential. Support in the form of short twiggy peasticks is necessary.

Propagation is by seed, stem cuttings and division. **Flowering** from June to August for *C. recta*; August to September for the others.

Family LILIACEAE *Colchicum* species

C. autumnale, the autumn crocus, is also known as meadow saffron, and the source of a narcotic poison. This attractive little plant is a native of Europe, and is common in Britain. It produces its bright purple cup-shaped flowers, similar in form to the crocus but unrelated, naked from the earth to a height of 15 to 22 cm in autumn. The large lance-shaped leaves appear in spring and summer long after the flowers have faded and can smother small plants if not carefully positioned. *C. bornmuelleri* (possibly only a form of *C. speciosum*), a plant from Asia Minor, has pretty flowers of rosy lilac. *C. speciosum* produces flowers varying from clear rose to deep crimson-purple, each with a white throat. There are several named varieties, including a white-flowered form. All the above are autumn-flowering. Colchicums grow well in a rich, moist soil that is well drained.

Naturalized in shrubberies, and at the front of herbaceous borders companioned with the dwarf blue Michaelmas daisies, they are effective. Plant not later than August.

Propagation is by separating the corms as soon as the leaves have died down in July. **Flowering** from August to October.

Family SCROPHULARIACEAE *Collinsia* species

A genus of about 25 species of attractive hardy annuals mostly native to western North America. *C. bicolor* is the species most usually encountered flowering well under town conditions. It reaches 30 cm with flowers of which the upper part is white and the lower rose-purple to violet. Colour variations occur. *C. bartsiaefolia* occasionally encountered is the seaside collinsia, and attains a height of 30 cm; the flowers are bell-shaped and white marked with lilac or purple. There are other forms with blue, violet and pink flowers. *C. grandiflora*, known as blue lips, has flowers with the upper part purplish-white and the lower deep blue or violet. *C. verna* is blue-eyed Mary, with flowers, the upper part white to purple and the lower bright blue.

Seed can be sown in autumn in well-drained lighter soils, or in late March or April, thinning to 10 cm apart. Cloche protection is not essential for autumn sowings, but may be advisable in severe winters, particularly with the early flowering *C. verna*.

Propagation is from seed. **Flowering** from midsummer onwards.

Lily-of-the-Valley

Family LILIACEAE *Convallaria majalis*

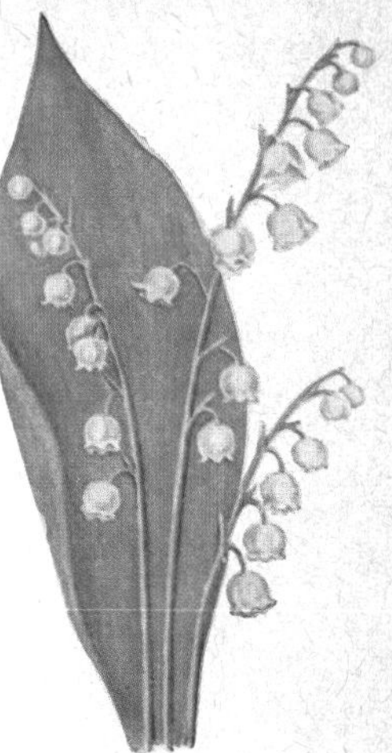

A native of Asia and Europe and occasionally found in England. The leaves and flowers grow from a creeping rootstock, the foliage being deep green in colour. The flowers are bell-shaped, 6 mm in diameter, pure white and deliciously fragrant and are carried on stalks, 15 to 30 cm high, from ten to twenty on each. They are followed by red berries in autumn. There are a number of forms, the most noteworthy being 'Fortin's Giant', a form selected for its larger flowers and strong fragrance. There is also 'Rosea', a form in which the white flowers are flushed pink, and the occasionally encountered taller-growing 'Prolificans'.

A well-drained rich loam containing coarse sand and a position in partial shade will grow them to perfection. September and October are the best months for planting. They should be allowed to form large clumps and, in the initial planting, should be placed 10 cm apart. When gathering the flowers give the stalks a sharp upward jerk and leave at least one leaf to each plant.

Propagate by division in September. **Flowering** May to June.

Convolvulus A

Family CONVOLVULACEAE *Convolvulus* species

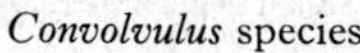

Natives of North America and the Mediterranean regions. The annual forms are to be preferred to those of perennial character as the latter often prove to be very difficult to control. The leaves are heart-shaped and the flowers funnel-shaped and wide open at the mouth; the habit either twining or spreading. The finest, *C. tricolor* (syn. *C. minor*), the dwarf morning glory from southern Europe, grows about 30 cm high, with 7·5 cm diameter blue flowers, with a yellow throat margined white. There are forms with various coloured flowers including 'Royal Marine', a dark blue dwarf form, 15 cm high; 'Royal Ensign', deep blue with golden centre; 'Crimson Monarch', cherry red. A perennial usually treated as an annual is *C. undulatus*, a twiner up to 120 cm with clusters of mid-blue flowers. One may encounter other plants in this family grown under the name convolvulus, but which are in fact of the genus *Ipomoea*.

All are easily grown from seed sown in well-drained soil in full sun in March.

Propagation is from seed. **Flowering** from June to September.

Tickseed

Family COMPOSITAE

Coreopsis species (annual)

A group of hardy annuals native to North America and sometimes listed as *Calliopsis* and *Leptosyne*, the former often being used to differentiate the annuals from the perennials. The leaves are mostly lobed or cut and the flowers borne singly or in panicles. The most noteworthy of the annual species is *C. tinctoria*, of which there are a number of strains from 15 cm to 1 metre in height including 'Tom Thumb Beauty', golden yellow with crimson centre, and 'The Garnet', with crimson-scarlet flowers. Other annual species: *C. atkinsoniana*, 60 to 120 cm, with flowers 3·7 cm across, orange with purple shading at the base; *C. calliopsidea*, reaching 60 cm, with golden-yellow flowers, 7·5 cm across; *C. coronata* (syn. *C. nuecensis*), 60 cm, having orange-yellow flowers, with a bronze-crimson zone, 5 cm across; *C. basilis* (syn. *C. drummondii*), 60 cm, with yellow flowers, 5 cm across, with a bronze-purple ring around a purple disc; 'Golden Crown' is a good strain.

Propagation is from seed. **Flowering** from midsummer until frost.

Coreopsis **P**

Family COMPOSITAE

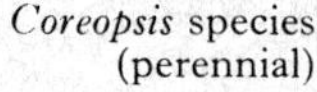
Coreopsis species (perennial)

Natives of North America and one of the most popular perennials, especially for cutting. *C. grandiflora* has lance-shaped leaves and slender branching stems 60 to 90 cm high, bearing flowers 6 cm across, broadly winged, and bright yellow in colour. 'Perry's Variety' is a double form. 'Badengold', golden-yellow and excellent for cutting, and 'Sunburst', a rich yellow, are good forms. 'Goldfink' is an attractive dwarf about 22 cm high, with deep yellow flowers. *C. verticillata* has fine feathery foliage surmounted by small yellow flowers. There is a form with larger flowers known as 'Grandiflora', 60 cm in height. *C. auriculata* has large flowers, yellow with a band of purplish-brown around the disc. *C. rosea*, 30 cm high, bears pale rose flowers.

Coreopsis are seen to best advantage towards the front of herbaceous borders near to purple or dark blue perennials of similar height.

Plant in spring or autumn in well-drained rich soil and allow to become established. Of the easiest culture.

Propagation is by division or seed. **Flowering** in late July and August.

Family COMPOSITAE *Cosmos* species

Our present garden forms of this genus have originated from three Mexican species and are among the most colourful of hardy annuals. The handsome *C. bipinnatus* has feathery foliage divided into linear segments and flowers, rather like single dahlias, crimson in colour with yellow centres. Garden varieties vary from white to mauve and pink: 'Sensation' varieties have large flowers with clear bright colours: 'Mandarin' has double orange flowers; 'Bright Lights' is a compact, mixed coloured strain growing to about 60 cm tall. With rather wider foliage, *C. sulphureus* reaches 90 to 130 cm, and bears large yellow, golden-centred flowers; its variety 'Sunset' has semi-double orange-red flowers.

The seed may be sown under glass in February or March, and the seedlings planted out in late May. If desired, it may be sown out of doors in late May for flowering in late summer. All are useful as cut flowers.

Propagation is from seed. **Flowering** from July onwards.

Montbretia **P**

Family IRIDACEAE *Crocosmia crocosmiiflora*

A hybrid of garden origin the result of a cross between the South African *C. pottsii* and *C. aurea*; often known as montbretia. The foliage is sword-like. The flowers are borne on branching leafy stems to a height of 60 to 90 cm. It is known mostly by its many beautiful varieties of garden origin, some having flowers up to 7·5 cm across and varying in colour from lemon yellow to orange, golden yellow and shades of scarlet and crimson; *C. masonorum*, about 90 cm high, flowers bright orange is perhaps the most spectacular species, hardy in milder areas in well-drained soils. There are also several hybrids of *C. masonorum* origin. May be grown in a well-drained rich soil containing ample humus, and the addition of well-decayed farmyard manure will add to the size of the individual flowers. Plant in March. On heavier soils lift in October and store under frost-proof conditions during autumn and winter.

Propagate in February by detaching the corms, potting in a leafy compost and planting in the open ground in May. **Flowering** in late summer.

Family IRIDACEAE *Crocus* species

A genus of a hundred or more species from the Mediterranean region and extending to south-west Asia. Foliage is narrow and grass-like. The flowers, funnel-shaped, are borne on long slender tubes; when extended they vary from 2·5 to 5 cm across. Among the spring-flowering species are *C. balansae*, orange-yellow, March flowering, *C. tommasinianus*, usually pale lavender, but variable; *C. chrysanthus*, S.E. Europe: bright yellow, but many varieties, some possibly of hybrid origin, in shades of yellow, white and blue; many striped. *C. biflorus*, varying from white to lavender and many large-flowered varieties generally termed Dutch crocus. Among those that bloom in autumn: *C. clusii*, from Spain and pale to deep purple; *C. longiflorus*, with fragrant flowers, rosy lilac with yellow base; and *C. nudiflorus*, clear violet, blooming in autumn before the foliage, which appears in spring, are noteworthy, but there are many others of garden value. Plant in late summer or early autumn in well-drained soil in sunny positions.

Propagate by separating the corms or from seed. **Flowering** from January to April for spring flowering and from September to December for autumn flowering forms.

Family PRIMULACEAE *Cyclamen* species

This genus of about twenty species is native to Central and southern Europe and countries bordering the Mediterranean. It includes both tender and hardy species. Of the hardy species *C. orbiculatum*, now usually regarded as a form of *C. vernum*, from the Caucasus and Asia Minor, reaches 7·5 cm high, having rounded leaves. The flowers vary from purple-rose to white, appearing from December to March. *C. europaeum* has purplish-red fragrant flowers; blooms from June to October. *C. ibericum* (also regarded as a form of *C. vernum*), the Caucasus, has white and purple flowers in late winter. *C. neapolitanum* has flowers pink or white in colour in August and September.

Cyclamen are shade lovers, and the corms should be planted in a leafy soil just below the surface; perfect drainage is essential and the introduction of limestone rubble is beneficial. Plant from June to November, and bed the base of each tuber in sand.

Propagation is from seed, sown immediately it is ripe, but can be done by cutting the old corms to pieces, each with an eye. **Flowering** varies according to the species, as detailed above.

Family COMPOSITAE *Dahlia cultivars*

A race of tuberous-rooted perennials found in Mexico and Guatemala. *D. pinnata*, and *D. rosea*, have been used in the evolution of the modern varieties. The characteristics of the cactus varieties are derived from *D. juarezii*. From these, and possibly other species, have arisen the present garden forms known as cactus, semi-cactus, pompon, decorative, collarette, etc. The plants vary in height from 30 cm to 2 metres or more. The flowers vary in size from 5 cm in diameter in the case of pompon varieties, to 38 cm in the case of large decorative varieties. They are mostly double in form, although some have single or semi-double flowers. They exhibit a wide range of colours with the exception of blue. There are many bicolour forms.

Dahlias will grow in any rich soil in full sun and with perfect drainage. As they are only half hardy, it is necessary to lift the tubers after the first autumnal frost, and dry and store in frost-proof conditions.

Propagation is by division of the tubers or by cuttings taken from tubers started into growth in February in heat, and rooted under glass. **Flowering** from July to September.

Family RANUNCULACEAE *Delphinium ajacis*

Annual delphiniums: *D. ajacis*, a native of the Swiss Alps, was one of the first species of these noble plants to be introduced to British gardens. Known also as the rocket larkspur, the foliage is finely cut and fern-like, and the stems attain 60 cm to 1 metre, with branching spikes of five sepalled florets, of single or double form, and varying considerably in colour from white to blue, violet, purple, pink and carmine. Good strains include the tall early-flowering hyacinth-flowered varieties and the 'Dwarf Rocket' strain, 30 cm in height. *D. grandiflorum* (syn. *sinense*) is often cultivated as an annual or biennial although a perennial. It reaches a height of 60 cm with very branching stems, bearing long-spurred florets of white or bright blue, 2·5 cm or more across, with small white centres sometimes shaded with blue. There are several named strains.

Annual larkspurs do not transplant satisfactorily; it is best to sow where they are to flower in September or March, and thin out when 2·5 cm or so high.

Propagate from seed. **Flowering** from July to September.

Delphinium

Family RANUNCULACEAE *Delphinium* species

The perennial delphiniums are a race of hardy plants widely distributed over the northern hemisphere. The foliage is elegantly lobed and divided, and the flowers borne in spikes on branching stems of various heights. *D. elatum*, reaching to a height of 1 to 2 metres, has spurred flowers of blue, 2·5 cm or less across and, with *D. cheilanthum* and *D. formosum*, is believed to have been the main influence in the evolution of the present-day magnificent garden varieties with flowers in many shades of blue and violet, white and pink. The 'Belladonna' hybrids are more compact in growth. *D. nudicaule*, from California, has scarlet florets on 45-cm high stems; *D. zalil*, a native of Iran, has pale yellow flowers. There are several other species in cultivation.

All require a deep, rich, well-manured soil in sun or partial shade, good drainage, and ample moisture during growth.

Propagate by means of division, cuttings or seed. **Flowering** in June and July, and again in late summer.

Pink **P B**

Family CARYOPHYLLACEAE *Dianthus* species

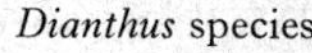

A race of perennials and annuals native to southern Europe, northern Africa and North America. The perpetual carnation grown in greenhouses is thought to be derived from crossing *D. caryophyllus* (the border carnation) and *D. sinensis* (the China Pink); the garden pink being derived from *D. plumarius.* The foliage varies in thickness and sometimes is as fine as coarse grass, glaucous green in colour. The flower-stems vary from 30 cm high in the case of pinks to a metre for carnations. The fragrant flowers are borne on the terminals of the stems in small quantities. Carnations are usually grown under glass, except border carnations, which may be grown out of doors. The pinks comprise such groups as the Allwoodii, Show and Imperial. Varieties of the laced type, also 'Mrs. Sinkins', 'Inchmery', and 'White Ladies', are old favourites. *D. chinensis* is the Indian or Chinese pink with a wide range of colour and grown as a half-hardy annual. *D. barbatus* is the popular sweet william which flowers in clustered heads.

Propagation is by cuttings, layering and seed. **Flowering** throughout the summer.

Family FUMARIACEAE *Dicentra* species

Natives of North America or eastern Asia, also called lyre flower or lock and keys. The perennial species of this genus now in cultivation are the old garden favourite *D. spectabilis*, from Siberia and Japan, at one time known as *dielytra*, with elegant, finely cut foliage and bearing on 60-cm arching stems pendent flowers, heart-shaped, deep rose, with inner petals of white that protrude conspicuously. There is a white-flowered form, 'Alba'. *D. eximia* and *D. formosa* have finer foliage with smaller flowers of rose. 'Bountiful' is a selected form of *D. formosa* with deep rose-pink flowers. 'Spring Morning' has light pink flowers. *D. eximia* 'Adrian Bloom' has crimson flowers. *D. chrysantha*, known as golden eardrops, reaches a height of 1 metre and bears golden yellow flowers—rather a rarity.

A rich light soil in partial shade will suit these easily grown plants admirably and a large established clump is most attractive. *D. spectabilis*, long cultivated in Britain, is often used for forcing under glass.

Propagation is by means of division of the roots when growth appears, or root cuttings. **Flowering** in spring.

Burning Bush **P**

Family Rutaceae

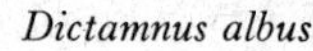

Dictamnus albus

One species alone is known with variations and is native to the region from South Europe to North China. The old garden favourite *D. albus*, once known as *D. fraxinella*, has glossy, leathery foliage with metre-length stems, bearing terminal racemes of fragrant flowers, somewhat like the Peruvian lily (q.v.) in form, but rather smaller, and white in colour; occasionally other colour forms may be encountered. The whole plant has the strong aroma of lemon. On the upper stem are glands which produce a fragrant, very volatile oil. This will ignite if a lighted match is held beneath the flowers during hot, still weather, the plant remaining unharmed. From this derives the name 'burning bush'. A good strong loam is best for these plants, and a position in full sun where it will become one of the most permanent of perennials, having been known to outlive several generations.

Propagate by seed immediately when ripe, its powers of germination waning very rapidly if stored for later sowing. Alternatively by division in March. **Flowering** in early summer.

Foxglove

Family SCROPHULARIACEAE *Digitalis* species

There are biennial and perennial forms of foxglove. *D. purpurea* is a biennial, sometimes perennial, a native of western and Central Europe, including Britain and Scandinavia. The leaves are large, ovate and downy. The flower-stems vary from 60 to 150 cm, bearing many slightly drooping tubular flowers open at the mouth, varying in colour from rose-purple in the wild form, to shades of pink, salmon, cream and white, all spotted, in the cultivated strains. The best known of these are the 'Excelsior' strain, and 'Foxy' strain—a strain that can be treated as hardy annuals. There is also a pure white unspotted form of particular beauty, 'Alba'. Occasionally plants produce flat, saucer-shaped (peloric) blooms at the tip of the spike. Useful for cutting. *D. lutea*, yellow flowers, about 60 cm high, is an attractive European species. *D. ambigua*, also European, has yellow flowers netted with brown.

Seed is best sown on a shady border in April outdoors, seedlings being transplanted to shady nursery beds, 7·5 cm apart, in June, and finally transferred to flowering positions in September to October.

Propagate from seed. **Flowering** in summer.

Family COMPOSITAE *Doronicum* species

The genus contains over twenty species native to Europe and temperate Asia, a few being useful and attractive garden plants, providing an early splash of yellow in the herbaceous border. In *D. plantagineum* the leaves are oval and toothed with leafy stems, 60 cm high and bearing yellow, daisy-like flowers, 7·6 cm across. The form 'Harpur Crewe' (syn. *D. p. excelsum*) has golden yellow flowers 2·5 cm larger than the type and is more robust in growth, usually about 1 metre in height. *D. caucasicum*, found in both Asia and Europe, has kidney-shaped leaves, deeply toothed. 'Miss Mason' is a bright yellow form about 60 cm in height; 'Spring Beauty', a good double-flowered form growing to about 45 cm.

The requirements of these plants are a reasonably deep fertile soil, well-drained but remaining moist during the growing season. Tolerant of sun or semi-shade; avoid sunny situation on drier soils.

Propagation is by division of the root in October or when growth begins in early spring. **Flowering** from April to early June.

Family COMPOSITAE *Echinops* species

The genus includes perennial species native chiefly to the Mediterranean region and the Middle East. They are rather coarse, erect-growing plants with decorative, bristly pinnate foliage of prickly lobes and teeth. The flower-heads are round, prickly and thistle-like in appearance. *E. ritro* with heads of steely-blue flowers on 1-metre stems, is the species most commonly encountered. *E. bannaticus* has greyish-blue heads on 60- to 90-cm stems; *E. nivalis* has white heads; *E. sphaerocephalus* has large heads of white and reaches as high as 1·5 to 1·8 metres. Good named forms derived from the above species include 'Blue Cloud', 'Taplow Blue', and 'Veitch's Dwarf Blue'. These plants provide soft colours that are valuable for toning down the more garish flowers. They are splendid in association with pink hollyhocks and *Gypsophila paniculata* 'Flamingo'. As cut flowers they lend themselves to many effective arrangements.

They are easily grown in any good, well-drained soil in full sun or partial shade.

Propagation is by means of root cuttings. **Flowering** from July to September.

Family RANUNCULACEAE *Eranthis hyemalis*

A dwarf perennial with a tuberous rootstock native to Europe, with related species in Asia. The leaves are immediately beneath the five- to eight-sepalled yellow flowers, borne on 15-cm stems. *E. hyemalis* grows well in any well-drained soil and appreciates the presence of a little leaf-mould or peat. *E. cilicica*, a species from Asia Minor, has more finely cut foliage than *E. hyemalis*, and with a bronzy tint. Flowers are a deep yellow with a stout stem. *E.* × *tubergenii* is a hybrid between the above two species. One of the best of the varied forms arising from this cross is 'Guinea Gold'. Among shrubs, in woodland, naturalized in short tuft and at the front of herbaceous borders it will be among the first of plants to show its flowers in the New Year. When planted in autumn it is well to allow the roots to remain undisturbed for a number of years when the flowers will form an effective carpet of golden yellow. It is advisable to plant thickly, 7 to 10 cm apart and about the same depth.

Propagate by lifting the tubers when dormant in summer, dividing and replanting; seed sown as soon as ripe will remain dormant until the following spring. **Flowering** from January to March.

Foxtail Lily

Family LILIACEAE *Eremurus* species

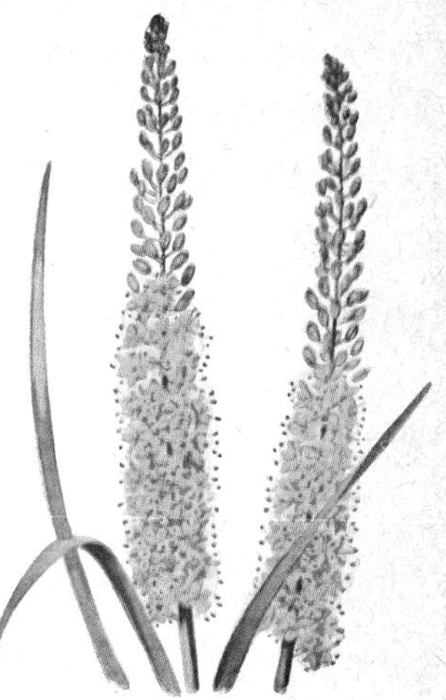

A genus of about thirty imposing and attractive perennials from the steppes of West and Central Asia. The foliage is linear. The individual flowers are numerous, usually yellow, white or pink, but of varying colours in hybrid strains, carried on tall, leafless spikes. *E. stenophyllus* (syn. *E. bungei*), native to Iran, has bright yellow flowers in 60-cm spikes. There are several colour forms. *E. himalaicus*, has white flowers, with bright orange anthers, in 1·8- to 2·4-metre spikes. *E. olgae*, from Iran and Northern Afghanistan, produces 1·2-metre spikes of rose-tinted white flowers, or pink flowers, in July. There are several good hybrids including a strain known as the 'Highdown Hybrids' with an extensive range of colour forms.

Eremurus are fairly hardy but require a well-drained soil and warm, sunny, sheltered position. Protection of the crowns with a mulch of bracken or leaves in winter is advisable to guard against spring frost damage of early growth.

Propagation is by division of crowns in August/September when dormant, or by means of seed. **Flowering** in July.

Flea-bane **P**

Family COMPOSITAE *Erigeron* species

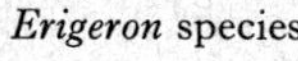

A genus of plants not unlike dwarf Michaelmas daisies, comprising both herbaceous and alpine species, widely distributed throughout the world. *E. speciosus*, from the western coast of North America, has a dwarf habit with short, narrow foliage and daisy-like flowers on 45- to 60-cm stems, of purplish lilac, about 5 cm across, with a yellowish disc at the centre. *E. macranthus*, of similar but neater habit, reaching about 45 cm, bears freely large purple flowers, yellow centred. *E. mucronatus*, a native of Mexico, is of compact habit, 22 cm high, and over a long period bears masses of pink flowers that fade to white. A great many hybrids have been raised, including 'Dignity', violet-mauve, 'Prosperity', light blue, 'Gaiety', deep pink, 'Festivity', lilac pink, 'Quakeress', pale blue, 'Darkest of All', deep purple.

A normal garden soil that is well drained and a position towards the front of the border in full sun will grow these easily cultivated plants to perfection. The flowers are useful for floral arrangements.

Propagation is by division of the roots in late summer or in March, species by seed. **Flowering** in June and July.

Sea Holly

Family UMBELLIFERAE *Eryngium* species

A race of perennials mostly to be found in Europe and the Mediterranean region. The blue-green foliage is deeply lobed and spiny with branching leafy stems and flower-heads similar in form to those of the teazel, enclosed in finely cut spiny bracts. The foliage varies in size, according to the species. *E. amethystinum*, Europe, reaches a height of 45 cm with flower-heads of metallic blue; *E.* × *oliverianum*, thought to be derived partly from *E. giganteum*, originated in the eastern Mediterranean and is 60 cm to 1·2 metres in height with highly coloured blue flower-heads; *E. alpinum*, Europe, reaches 30 to 60 cm, and possesses heads of bright metallic blue. *E. variifolium* has dark green leaves attractively marked with white; flowers small, blue. *E. planum*, from eastern Europe, is 60 cm high with roundish blue heads. *E. bourgati*, an over-all silvery blue, grows to about 45 cm. *E. tripartitum* is steely-blue with large bracts. 'Jewel' and 'Spring Hills' are amongst several named forms.

The Eryngiums are easily grown in any well-drained soil. The flowers are good for cutting and drying.

Propagation is by division, root cuttings and seed. **Flowering** from July to September.

Californian Poppy **A**

Family PAPAVERACEAE *Eschscholzia* species

A race of hardy annuals of brilliant colouring and of Californian origin. The most important species is *E. californica*, from which have originated the horticultural varieties that enjoy so much favour today. The plant grows 30 to 45 cm high, with finely cut glaucous green foliage and slender stems. It bears flowers, 7·5 cm across, that are yellow to orange in the type, but in the numerous named strains originating from this species, varying from golden yellow to carmine, coral, vermilion, and orange-scarlet, some with double flowers. 'Art Shades' and 'Mission Bells' are good dwarf strains about 22 cm high. The individual flowers are short lived but soon succeeded by others. *E. caespitosa* is a pretty dwarf, 15 cm high, with bright yellow flowers, 5 cm across. The seed should be sown in August or April, in a sunny, well-drained border where the plants are to bloom, and the seedlings thinned to 10 cm apart. Not suitable for a cut flower but effective in the mass.

Propagation is from seed. **Flowering** from midsummer to Michaelmas.

Family ROSACEAE *Filipendula* species

A genus of hardy herbaceous perennials native chiefly to Europe and Asia. *F. hexapetala*, dropwort, is an elegant plant with slender stems of 30 to 45 cm that carry branching sprays of small creamy-white flowers. *F. ulmaria*, the queen of the meadow or meadowsweet, native to Britain, Europe and many parts of Asia, has creamy-white sweetly scented flowers in long feathery plumes; 'Flore Pleno' has double flowers; 'Aurea' has golden yellow foliage. *F. palmata* (syn. *F. purpurea*) carries spreading plumes of purplish-pink flowers on metre-length stems. It has a white form, var. *alba*. *F. rubra* (syn. *Spiraea lobata*) has peach-pink flowers on similar stems. Its form 'Venusta' has deeper pink flowers. 'Magnifica' with the deepest pink flowers grows 1·2 to 1·5 metres high. *F. camtschatica* 'Rosea', 1·2 to 2 metres high, is an excellent plant for moist situations. These plants are related to but distinct from the shrubs of the genus *Spiraea*. They will grow in ordinary soils, but prefer moist conditions, except dropwort.

Propagate by division in spring. **Flowering** is June to August.

Fuchsia P

Family ONAGRACEAE *Fuchsia* species

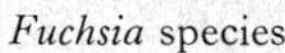

A colourful genus, comprising about a hundred species mostly native to tropical America, with a few in New Zealand. Shrubby plants with opposite oval leaves clothing stems that vary in height and bear flowers with recurving sepals, the petals forming a tube from which the stigma and anthers protrude conspicuously. Of the hardy species that may be grown in mild localities out of doors, *F. magellanica* of Chile has several forms, notably 'Alba', white-flowered, 'Gracilis', scarlet and purple, var. *pumila*, scarlet. From it also originates the hybrid '*Riccartonii*'. Several other hybrid fuchsias have proved fairly hardy, including 'Mrs. Popple' and 'Tom Thumb'.

They may be grown in the open border or, better still, against a south wall in good well-drained loam. Fuchsias are often cut to ground-level by hard frost, but invariably produce fresh growth and bloom freely in the same year.

Propagation is by means of cuttings of half-ripened wood in late summer. **Flowering** from June to October.

Family COMPOSITAE *Gaillardia* species

A native of North America and renowned for the brilliant colouring of its flowers, the perennial *G. aristata* has narrow, deeply lanceolate leaves, with stems up to 45 cm and flowers 10 cm across, comprising ray florets of orange-yellow and a zone of bronze-red surrounding a cone of blackish-brown. Good forms include 'Goblin', compact, 15 cm, cardinal red tipped lemon yellow, 'Mandarin', red tipped deep yellow, 'Burgundy', deep red, and 'Wirral Flame', orange-red.

Towards the front of the border in well-drained but rich soil gaillardias will provide a mass of brilliant colour over a long period that will be difficult to surpass; some of the forms may attain a metre or more in height. The gaillardia is particularly useful as a cut flower.

Propagation is by division, root cuttings or from seed. **Flowering** from June to October. *G. pulchella*, with yellow ray florets, purple at the base, is the best of the annual species. There are also several good annual strains, including 'Indian Chief' with single orange flowers, 'Lollipops', ball-shaped flowers, and 'Lorenzo' strain, both mixed colours.

Family AMARYLLIDACEAE *Galanthus* species

A lovely bulbous native of Europe and Asia Minor. The leaves are narrow and strap-shaped, and the stems, free from foliage, carry drooping flowers composed of three outer white spoon-shaped segments and three smaller inner ones that form a short corona, white and edged with green. Our native *G. nivalis* is familiar to all, and is one of the most cherished of our native plants, the flowers being borne singly from January to March on stems up to 22 cm; there are many forms, including *lutescens*, with a yellow edging to the corona instead of green, 'Sam Arnott', a form which increases well, and also a double-flowered form; the length of the outer segments is usually a little less than 2·5 cm. *G. elwesii* and *G. byzantinus* have larger flowers and reach a height of 25 to 30 cm.

The bulbs should be planted in late summer or early autumn in well-drained soil and they prefer heavier soils to light dry soils. Most prefer a semi-shady situation. They can be given a ground planting of one of the prostrate growing thymes to prevent the purity of the flowers from becoming marred by mud splashes.

Propagate by offsets when lifting the bulbs, or by careful division of clumps immediately after flowering. **Flowering** from January to March.

Family GERANIACEAE *Geranium* species

A genus of well over a hundred species of perennial herbaceous plants, occasionally sub-shrubs, distributed widely throughout the temperate regions of the world. Not to be confused with the bedding or fancy geraniums which belong to the genus *Pelargonium*. Several are native to or naturalized in Britain, growing in meadows or at the edge of woodlands. Leaves palmately lobed or divided, flowers borne in clusters on short stems rising from the densely leafy clumps. *G. ibericum*, from the Caucasus, reaches about 60 cm and flowers are violet-blue; *G. endressii*, from the Pyrenees, 30 to 45 cm high, has light rose-pink flowers, veined with deeper pink, 'Wargrave Variety' being a good darker form. *G. sanguineum* var. *lancastriense* has clear pink flowers and is little more than 15 cm high. 'Johnston's Blue', a hybrid up to 80 cm tall, has bright blue flowers.

The hardy geraniums will tolerate most soil conditions but prefer good drainage. They usually thrive in sun or shade.

Propagation is by division; the species from seed. **Flowering** from May to September.

Family Rosaceae *Geum* species

A genus comprising both alpine and taller forms common to temperate regions. The leaves are oblong and lobed, and form a rosette from which rise slender stems, bearing single or double flowers. The most important species is *G. chiloense*, a native of Chile, known also but erroneously as *G. coccineum*. Of its variations 'Grandiflorum', with double flowers, 38 mm across, several to a stem and reaching a height of 45 cm, is probably responsible for the popular varieties 'Mrs. Bradshaw', red semi-double, 'Lady Stratheden', yellow semi-double, and 'Prince of Orange', orange-yellow, double. *G. montanum* has flowers of rather less size, and the effective orange-flowered hybrid *G.* × *heldreichii*, reaching a height not exceeding 30 cm, is believed to owe its origin to this species. *G.* × *borissi*, a hybrid of garden origin, has rich orange-scarlet flowers.

Geums are among the easier of border perennials to cultivate and, provided they are given a position in full sun and a soil that is rich and well drained, no difficulties are to be expected in their cultivation.

Propagation is by means of seeds or division. **Flowering** from early summer onwards.

Family IRIDACEAE *Gladiolus* species

A genus comprising many cormous-rooted plants native to South Africa, and two to Europe. The leaves are erect and sword-like and the funnel-shaped flowers are of variable size, being borne on spikes that vary considerably in height. There are many named hybrids or forms in cultivation, in a wide range of colours. The 'Butterfly' strain is particularly notable for its symmetrical small-flowered spikes, valuable for cutting. *Primulinus* hybrids have hooded flowers. Species occasionally encountered: *G. byzantinus*, from Asia Minor, reaches 60 cm, bearing purplish-red flowers; *G. primulinus*, from south-east Africa, up to 1 metre, with small, hooded primrose-yellow flowers; *G.* × *colvillei* hybrids have medium-sized flowers varying from white to shades of pink or scarlet. *G. byzantinus*, *G. primulinus* and *G.* × *colvillei* can be planted deeply in late autumn in rich, well-drained soils in full sun where they may often establish and thrive. Alternatively plant early March. Plant hybrids March to May for successional flowering. Lift and store in frost-free conditions over-winter.

Propagate by cormlets and seed. **Flowering** from June to August.

Godetia **A**

Family ONAGRACEAE *Godetia grandiflora*

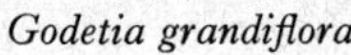

A genus of hardy annuals, related to *Oenothera*, that comes from California. *G. grandiflora* (syn. *Oenothera whitneyi*, *G. whitneyi*), from which our garden varieties have largely originated, has oblong leaves, up to 3 cm long, and stems 30 to 60 cm high that bear flowers up to 10 cm across varying in hue from white to rose red, blotched darkly at the centre. Of the varieties of garden origin '*Azaleaflora Plena*' has large double flowers of pink with crimson centres. 'Sybil Sherwood' has bright pink flowers, edged white; 'Whitney' is a hybrid strain with variously named colour forms, e.g. 'Crimson Glow', 'Lavender Queen', 'Orange Glory'. There are others of crimson, white, salmon, cerise, rose, cream-pink; some are dwarf and do not exceed 15 cm in height. Varieties varying in height from 38 to 60 cm, with single, semi-double and double flowers in a wide range of colour are available.

May be sown where plants are to flower in autumn or spring; or raised from sowings under glass, temperature 12° C to 18° C, in early spring. Fine for cutting.

Propagation is from seed. **Flowering** from late June to October.

Family CARYOPHYLLACEAE *Gypsophila* species

A genus which includes hardy perennials native to Europe and Asia, showy and effective for garden display. The most important species is *G. paniculata*, sometimes known popularly as baby's breath, with short, narrow, strap-like leaves about 7 to 10 cm long at the base of the plant and shortening as they clothe the lower part of the very branching slender stems. The flowers are single, white and small, produced in effective masses to a height of a metre or more but the double forms 'Pleno' and 'Bristol Fairy' are usually preferred. 'Rosy Veil' ('Rosenschleirer') is of more compact growth, with double pink flowers. 'Pink Star' has slightly darker flowers. Gypsophila grows well in most garden soils, provided there is ample drainage. The presence of lime is desirable.

Propagation is effected, in the case of single varieties, by seed, and by grafting on stocks of the type or by cuttings or root cuttings in the case of the double forms. **Flowering** during summer.

G. elegans is a hardy annual from the Caucasus. It has forms in white, carmine and rose-pink. The seed should be sown in April for later summer flowering.

Family Compositae *Helenium* species

A genus of about thirty species which includes annuals and perennials native to North America and Mexico; also called Helen flower or sneezeweed. Of erect growth, the leaves are lance-shaped and the flowers, several on a stem, are composed of wedge-shaped ray florets radiating from a central disc. *H. autumnale* is a tall species with varieties ranging from 60 cm to 2 metres and varying in colour from yellow to shades of chestnut-red. Hybrids originating from this species include 'Moerheim Beauty', mahogany-crimson, 'Butterpat', clear yellow, 'Wyndley', coppery-orange. 'Bressingham Gold', 'Bruno' and 'Coppelia' are other good garden forms. *H. bigelovii*, from California, reaches 1 metre with a central brown disc with yellow rays of typical form, 5 to 7·5 cm across.

Heleniums are indispensable border plants and grow well in full sun or partial shade in any good garden soil that has been well cultivated.

Propagate by division of the roots in early autumn or spring, or from seeds. **Flowering** from July to October.

Family COMPOSITAE *Helianthus* species

The genus consists of about sixty species, mostly native to North America, and includes annual and perennial species. The annual sunflower is *H. annuus*. reaching up to 4 metres or more. Hybrid strains, both single and double-flowered, range from the normal yellow to creamy-white and maroon. The perennial *H. decapetalus*, of variable height, has stems reaching from 1·2 to 2 metres, bearing flowers, 7·5 cm across, with light yellow ray petals. There are various double forms of garden origin including 'Flore Pleno' and 'Loddon Gold' and a very large, single-flowered form 'Maximus', 1·5 to 2 metres tall. Easily grown in any well-drained, fertile soil and sunny position. *H. scaberrimus* (syn. *H. rigidus*) is one of the best perennial species, reaching a height of 1 to 2 metres. *H. salicifolius* is a very distinct species, reaching a height of 2·1 to 2·4 metres, branched at the top and bearing many medium-sized yellow flowers.

Propagation is by division in late winter. **Flowering** from July to September.

Family COMPOSITAE *Helichrysum bracteatum*

A half-hardy annual that is native to Australia. Reaching a height of 60 cm to 1 metre, the plant has oblong and pointed leaves. It has flowers with many petals clustered and often incurving towards a central disc. They are known as everlasting-flowers, straw-flowers and immortelles. If the stems are cut when the flowers are just fully opened, and hung with the heads downwards to dry, they will retain their colour and form for a long period. Numerous named varieties have arisen from the 'Monstrosum' or double-flowered form in a wide range of colours: white, yellow, pink, red, purple. Also mixed strains and dwarf strains, 30 to 45 cm in height, such as 'Dwarf Spangles'.

The seed is best sown under cloches in the open ground in March or, without protection, in April, and the seedlings thinned to appropriate distances. *Helichrysum* is probably more to be valued for its lasting qualities than as a garden plant.

Propagation is from seed. **Flowering** from July onwards.

Family COMPOSITAE *Heliopsis* species

The genus consists of about seven species, all native to North America, but two only appear to have entered our gardens. The plants, both in habit of growth and form of flower, have much in common with the helianthus. *H. scabra* has produced many variations of garden origin notably '*Incomparabilis*', with large semi-double orange-rayed flowers which are centred with yellow discs, the whole flower being 15 cm or more across, borne on stems of 90 cm to 1·2 metres, and 'Patula', golden yellow flowers on 1·2-metre high stems (regarded by some authorities as a species). There are a number of double forms of attractive appearance and useful for border planting. These include 'Golden Plume', saffron yellow, 'Light of Lodden', bright yellow, and 'Goldgreenheart', lemon-yellow shading to green at the centre. *H. helianthoides* (syn. *H. laevis*), 1·5 metres tall, has single yellow flowers up to 7·5 cm across.

These plants will grow well in soil that has been well cultivated, enriched with manure and well drained. Valuable plants for herbaceous borders blooming, as they do, over a very long period. Good on drier soils.

Propagation is by division in late winter. **Flowering** from July to September.

Cherry Pie **A**

Family BORAGINACEAE *Heliotropium peruvianum*

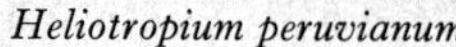

A native shrub of Peru, but tender and best treated as a half-hardy annual in Britain. Growing between 30 cm and 1·2 metres high, the plant is shrubby with oblong lance-shaped leaves and clusters of many violet or purple flowers, famous for their pronounced vanilla scent. *H. corymbosum*, a larger-flowered species, has also been cultivated in this country and from these two species have arisen the many forms, and perhaps hybrids, which in earlier years were widely used in summer bedding schemes. Commonly known as heliotrope. Few varieties are now grown, the most popular being 'Marina', deep violet-blue, 'Regale', a dark blue, very floriferous form.

The most successful method of culture consists in lifting plants from the open ground in September, wintering them in a warm greenhouse, and propagating new stock from cuttings in early spring.

Seed sown early in March will produce vigorous seedlings for planting out of doors in a sunny and well-drained position in early June. These will provide a good display in the same summer.

Propagation is from seed or cuttings. **Flowering** from midsummer onwards.

Hellebore

Family RANUNCULACEAE *Helleborus* species

A race of plants native to parts of Europe and western Asia. The foliage is deeply divided and of varying widths, according to the species. The familiar Christmas rose, *H. niger*, has large flowers of white, sometimes flushed with purple, on 22-cm stalks, and 7 to 10 cm across. 'Potter's Wheel' is a particularly fine form; 'Altifolius' a large early-flowering form. *H. viridus* has apple-green flowers and Lenten rose, *H. orientalis*, has flowers similar in size to those of *H. niger*, but varying in colour from purple and plum shades to purplish-pink, blush and pure or spotted white. *H. foetidus*, called the stinking hellebore from the unpleasant odour of its green and purple flowers, is a native.

These fascinating plants will thrive in any good garden soil in partial shade where sheltering evergreens may protect their blossoms from damage in wintry weather; the presence of leaf-mould in the soil is beneficial.

Propagate by division of the roots in early autumn or in spring. **Flowering** in autumn to early spring.

Family LILIACEAE *Hemerocallis* species

A race of colourful perennials that find their homes in Europe and Asia. The rush-like foliage is long and varies in width according to the species; the flowers which are borne on branching stems are like trumpet-shaped lilies in form and have the habit of lasting only for a day, being followed immediately by others. *H. flava* has 60-cm leaves with flower-stems up to a metre, bearing many pale ochre flowers. *H. aurantiaca* reaches to a metre, with six to eight bright orange flowers to each stem. *H. fulva* is about the same height, with yellow-orange flowers; there is also a double form. The Chinese *H. citrina*, 1·2 metres, has lemon-yellow flowers. There are many garden hybrids in shades of red, orange, yellow and pink, also bicolours.

By the side of streams or ponds where the roots may find the water without the plant becoming submerged, the day lily will grow satisfactorily as well as in the herbaceous border. A rich soil is necessary to grow them well as is also a position in full sun. Transplant in the spring just as growth begins.

Propagation is by division and from seed. **Flowering** from June to September.

Family SAXIFRAGACEAE *Heuchera* species

Of this genus there are about seventy species in all. They are natives of North America, and find their homes from Mexico to the Arctic regions. The leaves are heart-shaped, lobed and form a rosette at the base of the plant from which spring the slender flower-stems to 30 cm or more, bearing elegant panicles of flowers about 3 mm across. *H. sanguinea*, 30–60 cm, is the best known with red flowers, and various forms, and has, with *H. brizoides*, produced many hybrids, including 'Bressingham Hybrids', shades of crimson to pale pink, and 'Scintillation', purple-red. The bigeneric hybrid *Heucherella tiarelloides* is from a cross between *H. brizoides* and *Tiarella cordifolia*, having pale pink flowers. 'Bridget Bloom' is a good form. *H. americana* is the true alum root with dull purplish flowers.

Towards the front of the border and for cutting, the heucheras are among the most useful of plants. Well-drained garden soil, rich in humus and in full sun are suitable conditions.

Propagation is by means of division of the roots when growth begins, or from seed. **Flowering** in early summer.

Family LILIACEAE *Hyacinthus orientalis*

A genus of a few species only of bulbous-rooted plants found wild in the Mediterranean region and Asia Minor. The many varieties of the large florist's hyacinth used for spring bedding and for pot cultivation are derived from *H. orientalis.* In *H. orientalis* and its varieties the leaves are strap-shaped and the flowers are bell-shaped, 2·5 cm or more across, and borne in a dense raceme on thick stems up to 30 cm or more in height. The colour of the flowers can vary from white to yellow, orange, red, blue, pink and purple and are strongly scented. Hyacinths are produced very extensively in Holland where the plantations comprise pure sand into which has been introduced a liberal quantity of cow manure. Being quite hardy, hyacinths may be grown easily in well-drained soil. The time for planting is in late summer or early autumn. They are particularly well adapted for cultivation in bowls or pots, and specially pre-cooled bulbs may be brought into bloom by Christmas if given the requisite careful treatment and appropriate temperatures.

Propagation is by offsets or from seed. **Flowering** in April.

Family CRUCIFERAE *Iberis* species

A genus of annual and perennial species found in western Asia, southern Europe and northern Africa; all hardy in Britain. The perennials are shrubby, dwarf and compact. *I. sempervirens*, the common perennial candytuft, has snow-white flowers on 22- to 30-cm stems. 'Snowflake' and 'Little Gem' are named forms. *I. gibraltarica*, slightly larger, often has the flowers tinged red or lilac; flower stems often branched. For the front of the border these plants are pretty and effective. On the rock garden, too, they are effective if planted in bold colonies.

Propagation is by means of cuttings of half-ripened growth, seeds or root division. **Flowering** from April to July.

Of the annuals *I. umbellata* is dwarf with flowers in clustered heads, from white to bright shades of red and violet. Good strains include 'Dwarf Fairy', mixed colours, and 'Giant Pink'. Occasionally encountered *I. pectinata* (syn. *I. affinis*) has fragrant white flowers, fading to lilac; *I. amara* (syn. *I. coronaria*) has clusters of fragrant white flowers.

Propagation. Sow annuals in early April. **Flowering.** June to September.

Family GERANIACEAE *Impatiens* species

Natives of Africa and Asia, this genus comprises both hardy and half-hardy annuals and perennials. *I. holstii* is a tender perennial best treated as a half-hardy annual by raising from seed or cuttings under glass and planting out of doors in early June. The spurred flowers of scarlet, nearly 5 cm across, are on long stalks towards the tops of the stems. *I. sultanii* and *I. petersiana* are very similar to *I. holstii* and there are various hybrid strains. *I. roylei* (syn. *glandulifera*) is the old-fashioned big, coarse balsam of gardens, of erect habit, up to 2 metres, with purple flowers. It is naturalized in some areas, as is *I. noli-tangere*, an annual with red-spotted yellow flowers. *I. balsamifera* (balsam), a hardy annual species from India, with red flowers, is 60 cm tall. Its camellia-flowered strain is particularly attractive. It may be sown in April outdoors where the plants are to grow, but is best raised from seed sown under glass. Full sun and good drainage are essential.

Propagation is from seed or cuttings. **Flowering** season is from June to September.

Family BIGNONIACEAE *Incarvillea* species

A genus of showy perennials found in various parts of China and Central Asia. The foliage is elegant and fern-like, comprising many segments borne on stems sometimes 30 cm long. The flowers are trumpet-shaped, open at the mouth and 5 to 7·5 cm long, and of a similar width. *I. delavayi*, from China, carries up to twelve flowers of rosy-purple on 60-cm stems. 'Bee's Pink' is a good form. *I. mairei* var. *grandiflora*, from China, has its flowers either solitary or in pairs and of a deep rose shade. *I. olgae*, from Turkistan, has flowers of only 3·7 cm in length and a pretty pale pink shade. In order to enjoy the fine foliage and general elegance of a well-grown plant of incarvillea it is necessary to provide a light, sandy soil that has been enriched with decayed manure, and plant young stock from pots. The position should be warm and fully exposed to the sun, but protected from cold winds. It is wise to afford some protection during winter.

Propagate by division of the root in late winter or from seed. **Flowering** in May and June.

Family CONVOLVULACEAE *Ipomoea* species

These are mostly natives of tropical America, comprising both annuals and perennials, best treated as half-hardy annuals, also called moon creeper. *I. rubro-caerulea* (syn. *Pharbitis tricolor*) is the most favoured for outdoor cultivation with lovely clear blue flowers, 10 cm across at the mouth, and white in the tube. It climbs up to 2 metres and there are named strains with blue, pink or scarlet flowers. *Mina lobata* (syn. *I. versicolor*), closely related to *Ipomoea*, will climb up to 2 metres or more, with flowers that are crimson in bud, but change on opening to pale yellow. *Quamoclit pennata*, also closely related, 2 metres, has scarlet flowers and should be grown out of doors only in the warmest localities. *I. purpurea*, 2 to 2·4 metres, has flowers of purple, blue or pink and sometimes produces double flowers. For the outdoor flower garden *I. rubro-caerulea* is the most satisfactory and requires to be raised from seed sown early in the year under glass.

The seeds are best sown at the rate of two in a 10-cm pot as they do not prick off satisfactorily. Plant out against a sunny south wall or trellis in early June.

Propagation is from seed. **Flowering** from July to September.

Family IRIDACEAE *Iris* species

A genus found throughout the temperate regions. The bearded irises comprise hundreds of the garden varieties. The foliage is sword-like and the flowers, borne on 60- to 120-cm stems, have three upper or standard petals and three lower or fall petals. *I. kaempferi*, the Japanese water iris, has broad and flat-headed flowers of varied shades, and *I. sibirica*, also a water lover, is rather like a miniature flag. *I. unguicularis* (syn. *I. stylosa*) is from Algeria and the eastern Mediterranean and has rich deep-purple-blue flowers from November to March. The gladwyn (*I. foetidissima*) is noted for its brilliant orange seeds in autumn. The foregoing are all lime lovers. Of the bulbous iris there are the Dutch, Spanish and English types with narrow foliage and 60-cm stems, bearing flowers with long pedicels and 5-cm segments blotched yellow. *I. reticulata*, which blooms in February, suggests a miniature purple iris of this form.

Propagate by division in the case of bearded irises and by means of offsets in the case of bulbous species. **Flowering** mainly in June, but there are bulbous species that bloom in late winter and early spring.

Family VALERIANACEAE *Kentranthus* species

Some species are native to the Mediterranean region, but those usually seen in gardens are European. The foliage is lanceolate, smooth and glaucous, and the habit of the plant is compact. The flowers are small and borne in umbels about 5 cm across at the end of the 45-cm stems. They vary in colour from crimson to white, and are produced freely. *K. ruber*, its white form 'Albus' and its scarlet form 'Atrococcineus' are those most commonly found in gardens, and have been known in Britain for many years. *C. angustifolius*, occasionally encountered, reaches 60 cm with clear rose or white flowers of similar form. Both species are fragrant.

Cultivation is easy for the valerian grows in any soil and often naturalizes itself in the crevices of old walls and masses of the red form are commonly seen on railway embankments in the western counties.

Propagation is by means of division or seeds. **Flowering** through the whole summer.

The most attractive hardy annual of this genus is *K. macrosiphon*, a native of Spain infrequently encountered in cultivation. The seed should be sown in late March or April.

Family LILIACEAE *Kniphofia* species

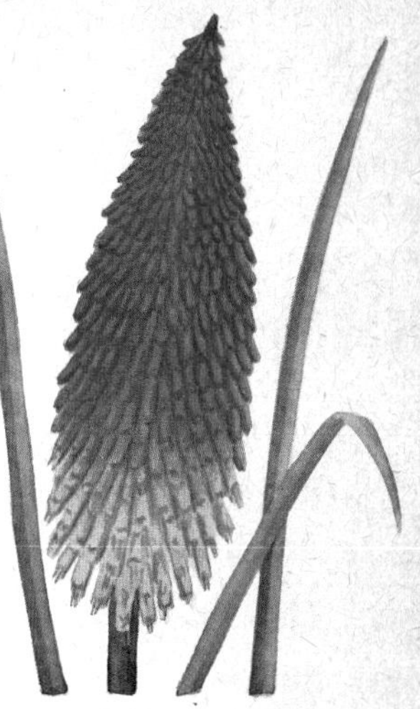

This genus hails from South Africa, and is also called torch lily. The foliage is long and reed-like. The flowers are borne on thick leafless stems, funnel-shaped and in dense racemes of varied size. *K. uvaria* (syn. *aloides*) will attain a height of 1·2 metres, bearing racemes 15 cm long of bright scarlet flowers changing to yellow in the lower portions. Var. *nobilis* will reach 2 metres in height. *K. rufa* is a smaller species, reaching 45 cm with primrose yellow spikes tinged red at the apex. *K. galpini* is of 60 to 90 cm, with apricot-coloured flowers. *K. nelsoni*, 60 cm high, has bright scarlet flower spikes, sometimes suffused orange. *K.* × *erecta* has scarlet flowers and is unique in that its flower-tubes turn upwards. *K. praecox*, up to 2 metres, with red and yellow flowers, is early flowering. Among garden hybrids 'Bee's Sunset', 'Maid of Orleans', 'Bressingham Torch' and 'Royal Standard' are particularly meritorious.

A rich soil in full sun is essential and planting is in April or May.

Propagate by division in spring or from seed. **Flowering** in summer and early autumn.

Sweet Pea **A P**

Family LEGUMINOSAE *Lathyrus odoratus*

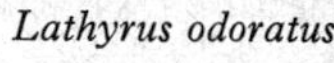

One of the most prized of all annuals. The original species is a native of Sicily, but it is to the many varieties of garden origin that the sweet pea owes its popularity. Of climbing habit, growing 2 to 3 metres high, *L. odoratus*, as its name suggests, is strongly fragrant, climbing by means of tendrils. The flowers are of the familiar keeled pea shape, two to seven or more on a stem, in a wide range of colour, including white and cream but as yet no true yellow. There are several low-growing strains, growing to little more than a metre in height, such as 'Knee High' and 'Jet Set', both mixed-colour strains. 'Little Sweetheart' is compact and bushy at 22 to 30 cm.

For ordinary garden cultivation, the seed may be sown in the later summer in pots, wintered in a cold frame and planted out in March in deeply cultivated ground that has been limed and well fed with organic manure. Peasticks or canes are necessary for support. Seed may also be sown in late March out of doors, spaced about 15 cm apart and given support. *L. latifolius*, the everlasting pea, is a hardy perennial, flowers white, pink or rosy-purple.

Flowering from midsummer onwards.

Family MALVACEAE *Lavatera* species

A genus of hardy shrubs and showy annuals. *L. arborea*, from southern Europe, in milder areas forms a shrubby plant, 2 to 3 metres high, with large lobed leaves, and flowers, of trumpet shape, 5 cm across, reddish-purple veined with a deeper shade at the base, in clusters. It can be grown as a biennial. *L. trimestris* (syn. *L. rosea*) grows 1 metre or more, is native to southern Europe, and an annual. The flowers are of a rosy-red shade. There are a number of varieties of garden origin, such as 'Alba', a good white form, 'Roseo Splendens', bright rose pink, 'Loveliness', a beautiful, rich deep rose pink and 'Sunset', darker still. *L. olbia*, the tree lavateria, is a perennial shrubby species growing to 2 metres. Leaves are soft and woolly, flowers similar in appearance to hollyhock are reddish-purple. 'Rosea', soft pink, is a good form.

Seeds of shrubby kinds may be sown in frames in early autumn, or in their flowering positions in April. The seed of the annuals may be sown out of doors in late March where the plants are to flower.

Propagation is from cuttings or seed. **Flowering** from midsummer onwards.

Family LILIACEAE *Lilium auratum*

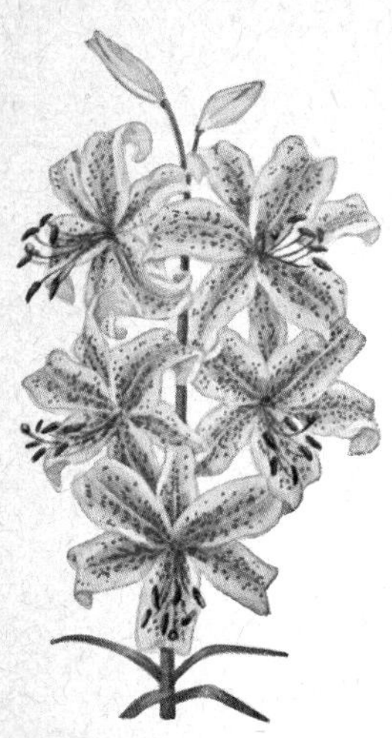

Widely considered the most beautiful of all lilies and a native of Japan. Reaching up to 2 metres high the leafy stems carry up to fifteen strongly fragrant flowers, 20 to 25 cm across. The colour is white, with a mid-rib of pale yellow the whole length of each segment, spotted crimson. Its form var. *platyphyllum* is of more vigorous growth of the same colour, but not so heavily spotted; var. *rubro-vittatum* is distinguished by a crimson band running the whole length of each segment, and the flowers are spotted crimson. There are other forms and a number of hybrid strains including 'Esperanza', 'Imperial Silver', 'Parkmanii' and 'Jamboree'. In a rich, peaty soil, well drained and free from unrotted animal manure, these lilies are seen to best advantage if planted in a sheltered position, sun or semi-shade in shrub borders, particularly among rhododendrons and azaleas where they effectively extend the period of interest for such plantings.

Propagate from scales, offsets or seed. **Flowering** in late summer, but the flowers may be forced earlier under glass.

Candlestick Lily

Family LILIACEAE *Lilium × hollandicum*

A popular and easily grown group of garden hybrids, often known as *L. umbellatum*, with leafy stems up to 1 metre tall, several flowers being borne in a terminal umbel, brilliant orange or red shades variously spotted purple and suffused yellow in the throat. There are many forms, such as 'Golden Fleece', bright yellow, 'Grandiflorum', orange, shading to red, 'Incomparable', rich crimson.

There are also other hybrid strains derived from *L. × hollandicum*, including the excellent 'Golden Chalice Hybrids', clear yellows to rich golden shades, 'Mid-Century Hybrids', with named forms such as 'Destiny', 'Enchantment' and 'Harmony', and the numerous forms of the hybrid group *L. × maculatum*. Plant with the shoulder of the bulb two and a half times the bulb's depth below the surface, with sharp sand below and above to aid drainage. Position amongst low-growing shrubs in sun or semi-shade, working in leaf-mould when planting and mulching with it annually.

Propagate by means of offsets, or bulb scales. **Flowering** in June and July.

Turk's Cap Lily P

Family LILIACEAE *Lilium martagon*

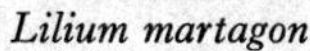

Mostly natives of the Old World, lilies of this group bear flowers of varying size, drooping with re-curved petals, hence the popular name. *L. martagon* is the turk's cap lily of southern Europe, with flowers of dull violet-rose, spotted carmine at the base and borne in candelabra-like tiers; var. *album* is pure white. *L. chalcedonicum*, the scarlet turk's cap, has flowers of brilliant vermilion-scarlet, slightly dotted purple. *L. testaceum* has flowers of a pretty yellow, flushed pink, and sweetly scented. *L. henryi* is a majestic plant up to 2·4 metres with up to twenty flowers of brilliant orange, slightly spotted brown, with a green band at the base of each segment; a native of Central China. *L. tigrinum*, the tiger lily, a native of China and Japan, reaches up to 1·2 metres, with flowers of deep orange-red, heavily spotted purple. The 'Marhan' hybrids offer a wide range of colour forms from buff to orange-yellow and maroon. They are derived from *L. martagon* and *L. hansonii*.

Plant to a depth equal to three times the diameter of the bulb in a soil rich in humus.

Propagate by offsets, scales, stem bulbils in the case of *L. tigrinum* and from seed. **Flowering** in summer.

Family PLUMBAGINACEAE *Limonium* species

A genus of wide distribution, formerly known as *Statice*, that includes several perennial species at home near sea coasts. *L. latifolium*, from south-eastern Europe, has oblong-elliptical, smooth leaves, tall branching scapes, carrying panicles of small blue flowers up to a metre tall. 'Blue Cloud' is a good form. *L. gmelinii*, from the Caucasus, has smooth ovate leaves, and 30- to 60-cm stems with panicles of deep purplish-blue flowers. *L. vulgare*, the common sea lavender of our own coasts, with purple flowers, grows about 30 cm high. *L. sinuata* is grown as an annual with flowers having blue calyces and yellowish-white corollas. There are strains which include yellow and pink flowers. *L. suworowii*, with pink flowers, is a hardy annual species. Culture is simple, for the plants are easily established in any well-drained, light or sandy loam. They like a sunny position.

Propagation may be done by root cuttings in early spring, by division or from seed. **Flowering** from July to September.

Family SCROPHULARIACEAE *Linaria* species

A genus native to Europe, North Africa and Canada, including many annuals and perennials. From Morocco we have *L. maroccana*, an annual of 22 to 30 cm, with narrow foliage and short spikes of small flowers that are violet-purple with yellow markings and pointed spurs. There are many charming garden varieties, bushy and compact, that produce flowers of white, yellow, purple, lavender, pink and violet-blue and mixed colour strains, e.g. 'Fairy Bouquet'. *L. bipartita*, from Portugal, has violet flowers with an orange lip. There are white, red, violet, rose, yellow and purple flowered forms. *L. vulgaris*, native to Britain, is a perennial of spreading habit bearing flowers like snapdragons in sulphur yellow with an orange lip. *L. purpurea*, perennial, blush-purple is naturalized in Britain. 'Canon Went' is a good form.

Seed may be sown in August or April where the plants are to flower, thinned to 10 to 15 cm apart. They like a sunny position and a well-drained humus-rich soil.

Propagation is from seed. **Flowering** in early summer, and later if plants are prevented from developing seed.

Family LINACEAE *Linum* species

A genus which includes several perennial species of considerable charm, native to Europe. The stems are slender and branching, and clothed from the base upwards with short, narrow, pointed grassy foliage. *L. perenne* has five-petalled flowers, 37 mm across, of lovely azure-blue, borne in profusion on branching stems up to 45 cm; it also has a white flowered form. *L. narbonense* has similarly sized flowers of azure-blue with an effective white centre and stamens, up to 60 cm high. 'Six Hills' is a good form. Less commonly seen are 30- to 45-cm species from eastern Europe, with golden yellow flowers, and '*Lewisii*', the prairie flax, from western America, a form of *L. perenne*.

Easily cultivated in any open position in full sun and useful for the base of rock gardens.

Propagation is by division or from seed. **Flowering** in late spring.

The annual variety *L. grandiflorum*, from Algeria, and its various colour forms, should be sown from March to June for June to September flowering.

Family CAMPANULACEAE *Lobelia* species

A widely distributed genus of hardy and half-hardy perennials, some being treated as annuals. The edging lobelia is *L. erinus*, from South Africa, a semi-trailing perennial, grown as a half-hardy annual, 15 to 22 cm high, with small rounded foliage and leafy stems, bearing many flowers. There are numerous named colour forms, e.g. 'Crystal Palace', 'Mrs. Clibran Improved', of crimson, pale blue or violet with a white or yellow throat, also white-flowered strains. *L. tenuior* (syn. *L. ramosa*), from West Australia, 30 to 45 cm, has blue flowers, 2·5 cm across. 'Compacta Improved' is a good form for colour schemes. *L. ilicifolia*, from Australia, is of trailing habit and is best known by its garden variety, 'Sapphire', which is useful alike for hanging baskets or rock gardens.

The seed should be sown in a leafy compost in either autumn or spring. If in autumn, greenhouse protection during winter is necessary. The seedlings are pricked off into boxes and planted out in late May or early June. It is wise to stop the seedlings when 2·5 cm high in order to encourage bushy growth.

Propagation is from seed or cuttings. **Flowering** from June to Michaelmas.

Family CRUCIFERAE *Lunaria annua* (syn. *L. biennis*)

A native of Europe and of biennial habit; known also as satin-flower, money-flower and moon-wort. The leaves are ovate and toothed and the stems attain a height of up to 1 metre, with the flowers, about 12 mm across and purple in colour, borne in branching sprays. There is a white-flowered form, 'Alba', a crimson form 'Atrococcinea', 'Munstead Purple' with rich purple flowers and 'Variegata' with leaves margined creamy white. The flowers are followed by flat, oval seed-pods, about 5 cm long, which, when the outer covering has been shed, reveal attractive silvery discs that are much prized, when dried, for use in winter decoration, sometimes being dyed various colours. *L. rediviva*, a perennial species with small fragrant purplish flowers, is the only other member of the genus.

Will grow well in any good soil in sun or partial shade, the seed being sown in the late summer for producing flowering plants for the following season. A pretty woodland plant.

Propagation is from seed, or with *L. rediviva*, division. **Flowering** from April to June.

Family LEGUMINOSAE *Lupinus* species

This North American genus is among the most important perennials. The foliage comprises five to fifteen long, narrow leaflets, 10 to 15 cm long, radiating from a short stem at the base of the plant and sometimes from the flower-stems. The flowers, borne in long spikes, 1 metre or more, comprise a lower portion pouch-shaped, known as the keel, and an upper petal that is recurved in the older types, but flat in the more modern strains, particularly the Russell strain. In the varieties of garden origin the shades vary from white to yellow, orange, flame, red, bronze, pink and intermediate shades as well as lavender-blue and purple. *L. hartwegii* is an annual species from Mexico, flowers blue with whitish keel. Height up to 1 metre. There are various strains including dwarf and mixed colour strains. *L. arboreus*, the tree lupin, is shrubby with shorter spikes of yellow, white or mauve.

Requires a well-drained rich soil and a position in partial shade or full sun.

Propagate by means of cuttings or from seed. **Flowering** in June, *L. hartwegii* to October.

Family CAROPHYLLACEAE *Lychnis* species

Lychnis coeli-rosea, (botanically, *silene*), from the Levant is a charming annual and worthy of a place in any garden. The plant grows about 30 cm high, with linear leaves and solitary terminal flowers, 2·5 cm across, of glowing rose and purple. There are various forms and from var. *oculata*, sometimes listed as *Viscaria oculata*, have originated garden forms with flowers of blue, white, carmine, pink and scarlet. *L. githago* (syn. *Agrostemma githago*) reaches 60 cm or more and is the native corn cockle of British cornfields with purplish-red flowers and long leafy sepals.

The seed should be sown in April on well-drained ground in sunny positions where the plants are to bloom, thinning to a few centimetres apart when the seedlings are 2·5 cm high. There are a number of perennial species including *L. chalcedonica*, *L. coronaria*, *L. flos-jovis* and the hybrid *L.* × *haageana*.

Propagation is from seed. Perennials by division.
Flowering from midsummer to Michaelmas.

Family PRIMULACEAE *Lysimachia* species

A genus of variable habit and comprising perennial herbs that inhabit moist places in the temperate and subtropical regions of the world. *L. nummularia* is the familiar creeping jenny of prostrate habit with slender stems clothed with rounded foliage and small yellow flowers; it will grow almost anywhere. *L. clethroides*, of Japan, reaches 1 metre, with large opposite foliage and white flowers, 12 mm across, borne in a long, slender terminal spike. A good species for cutting. *L. leschenaultii*, from India, with spikes of purplish-red flowers, reaches 30 cm. *L. fortunei*, from China and Japan, reaches 45 cm, with loose spikes of yellow flowers above elegant foliage. *L. punctata*, 60 to 90 cm, is a European with large yellow flowers, tinged reddish at the base. *L. ephemerum*, 90 cm, is a white-flowered species from South Europe. These are the leading species for use in gardens and are of the easiest cultivation, but prefer a damp situation to one where drought could cause damage. Tolerant of sun or shade.

Propagation is effected by division or from seed. **Flowering** season is in summer.

Family MALVACEAE *Malva* species

Malva moschata is a useful herbaceous perennial and native to Europe. The foliage is finely lobed and possesses the elegance of some ferns. The stems reach a height of 60 to 90 cm and are branching, bearing five-petalled flowers, 25 to 37 mm across, of rose; the calyx is hairy. There is also a white-flowered form, 'Alba', that is considered by many gardeners to be the most desirable of the species and is slightly musk-scented. These old garden plants may be seen growing wild at the side of roads and are easily cultivated in gardens, requiring no special cultivation but giving the best results in sun or partial shade. *M. alcea*, perennial, has rose-purple flowers, var. *fastigiata*, 1·2 to 1·8 metres, with darker flowers being the form usually grown. *Malope trifida*, closely related to the mallows, is an annual species, native of Mediterranean regions, growing to about 30 cm in height. Flower colour purple to white. 'Grandiflora' is a large-flowered strain.

Propagation is by means of seed sown in cold frames in March and planted out in May. **Flowering** is in summer.

Family CRUCIFERAE *Matthiola* species

Native to the Mediterranean region. *M. incana* of the Levant is the parent of the ten week stock; also the Brompton stock, sturdy biennials with flowers usually of purple, but the flower colour of various strains varies from white to blush, yellow, red and purple. From crosses made between *M. sinuata*, a British native, and other species, has originated the East Lothian stock, and the intermediate stock. *M. bicornis*, from Greece, is the night-scented stock. Of dwarf habit, this annual produces masses of small lilac-purple flowers.

The seed of *M. incana* is sown under glass in April and the plants placed in their permanent positions in May or June. *M. sinuata* should be raised from seed sown under glass in September, being pricked off into boxes and planted out in April.

Propagation is from seed. **Flowering** season of stocks is very extensive and by careful selection and cultivation of the various strains, plants can be had in bloom throughout the year.

Family PAPAVERACEAE *Meconopsis* species

A genus mostly native to Asia. *M. betonicifolia* (syn. *M. baileyi*), the blue Tibetan poppy, has stems up to 90 cm, bearing several brilliant peacock-blue flowers centred with orange stamens. It is usually perennial only if the flower-buds are removed in the first season before flowering. *M. cambrica*, the Welsh poppy, a native of western Europe, reaches 30 cm high, with yellow poppy-like flowers, 5 cm across. One of the most popular species is *M. integrifolia*, the Tibetan lampshade poppy, with spikes of pale yellow poppy-like flowers, up to 15 cm across. It is monocarpic. *M. dhwojii*, from the Himalayas, is also yellow-flowered. *M. regia* has bright yellow flowers on stems up to a metre or more. *M. grandis*, monocarpic, 90 cm, from Nepal, has violet- or slate-blue flowers, and *M. quintuplinervia*, 30 to 45 cm, is a dainty Tibetan, with flowers of lilac-blue.

These plants, except *M. cambrica* which will grow in ordinary sandy loam, require partial shade and lime-free soil rich in peat or leaf-mould and well drained.

Propagate from seed. **Flowering** in spring.

Family AIZOACEAE *Mesembryanthemum* species

Colourful half-hardy succulents of South African origin and admirable for dry and sun-baked soils. *M. criniflorum*, growing 10 cm tall, has succulent leaves, about 7·5 cm long, widening from a narrow base, with a spreading habit well adapted to covering dry walls, and flowers of daisy-like form in brilliant shades of pink, red, white, yellow and orange. *M. gramineum* (syn. *M. tricolor*) is of similar habit, flowers white, pink, purple or rose, with dark centres. Hardier is the ice plant, *M. crystallinum*, with fleshy stems and a spreading habit, comprising 15-cm oval, pointed leaves and many small flowers of white or rose-pink shades; a useful wall or edging plant. *Carpobrotus edulis* (syn. *M. edulis*) from Cape Province, commonly called Hottentot fig, is naturalized in some milder areas of Britain, including Cornish sea cliffs. Flowers are large, 7 to 10 cm across, yellow or purple. The fruit is edible. Except in the mildest climates it is wisest to sow a few seeds in small pots under glass in March, grow on under protection and plant out direct from the pots into a well-drained soil that enjoys full sun in June.

Propagation is from seed. **Flowering** from midsummer until frost.

Monkey-flower

Family SCROPHULARIACEAE *Mimulus* species

A race which includes many moisture-loving perennial herbs found chiefly in North America, but some are from Africa, Asia and Australasia. The leaves vary from oblong to lance-shaped with serrated edge. *M. luteus* can vary in height from 30 to 45 cm with flowers comprising two upper and three lower lobes of deep yellow with dark blotches, the corolla being from 2·5 to 5 cm long. *M. cupreus*, similar to *M. luteus*, but more tufted, has coppery-orange, yellow-throated flowers. From these two species have originated numerous forms and hybrids e.g. 'Fireflame', 'Red Emperor', 'Whitecroft Scarlet'. *M. cardinalis* reaches 30 to 60 cm, with scarlet flowers. *M. moschatus*, naturalized in parts of Britain is the musk plant with creeping roots and stems up to 15 cm, bearing small pale yellow flowers lightly spotted brown. *M. lewisii*, 30 cm, with rose flowers, is from north-west America. In the moister parts of herbaceous borders, and in some shade, these plants are easily grown.

Propagate by division, cuttings, or from seed. **Flowering** continuous throughout the summer.

Family NYCTAGINACEAE *Mirabilis jalapa*

A perennial from tropical America but, being unable to withstand winter frosts, is best treated as a half-hardy annual. The species develops into a shapely plant up to 90 cm, with five-lobed tubular fragrant flowers 2·5 to 5 cm long, red, yellow, white and often mottled. Its habit of opening in the afternoon has gained for it a further popular name of four-o'clock. Slightly taller and more branching is *M. multiflora*, bearing clusters of rose or purple flowers, 5 cm long. Occasionally encountered, *M. longiflora* reaches 90 cm with white, rose or violet flowers, 10 to 15 cm long, and *M. dichotoma*, 75 cm high, has flowers of white heavily suffused with pink and effectively contrasting purple stamens.

Seed should be sown under glass in March, and the seedlings pricked off and planted out when all risk of frost has passed. A position in full sun and a well-drained soil are essential.

Propagation is from seed. Tuberous roots may be treated as for dahlia, lifting in autumn, drying and storing over-winter in frost-free conditions. **Flowering** from midsummer until frost.

Family LILIACEAE *Muscari* species

A large genus of attractive hardy bulbous plants, native variously to Europe and Asia Minor. The foliage rises from the bulb and consists usually of narrow, linear leaves, rather fleshy and untidy in the mass. The flowers are small, of rounded shape, constricted at the mouth, and borne in close spikes; hence the name of the most popular species *M. botryoides,* meaning 'like a bunch of grapes'. The individual flowers are of a deep sky-blue shade, with six white-toothed segments; there are also pale blue and white forms, all of erect habit up to 22 cm. *M. armeniacum* flowers later than most, reaches 20 cm, with racemes 10 cm long of bright clear blue flowers with white segments. Good named forms are 'Blue Spike' and 'Cantab'. *M. racemosum,* 15 cm, has deep purple flowers. *Leopoldia* (*Muscari*), *comosa* 'Plumosa', 20 cm is the feather hyacinth and has soft violet-flowers.

Massed in the front of herbaceous borders, beneath deciduous shrubs and in sparse woodland, these are among the most charming of spring flowers. Plant in autumn in well-drained soil.

Propagate by division, by offsets or seeds. **Flowering** in spring.

Family BORAGINACEAE *Myosotis* species

A genus of pretty annuals and perennials, which are mostly native to Europe, also known as scorpion grass. *M. alpestris* (syn. *M. pyrenaica*) is the Alpine forget-me-not; up to 20 cm high, with lovely blue flowers. 'Blue Ball', 'Carmine King', 'Indigo', 'Rosea', 'Warley Blue' and 'Ultramarine', are good forms. *M. dissitiflora*, 20 to 25 cm, is long flowering, with dark sky-blue flowers from May to July, and has a white form 'Alba'. *M. sylvatica* (syn. *M. oblongata*) is a native with branching stems and blue flowers centred with yellow. There are also white, pink and striped forms. *M. scorpioides* (syn. *M. palustris*) is the true forget-me-not with bright blue, yellow-eyed flowers, but a plant variable in size and colour, including a white form, 'Alba', and 'Semperflorens' a dwarf, long-flowering form. *M. caespitosa*, 7·5 to 15 cm, forms dense blue-flowered cushions. There are also several selected hybrid strains of *Myosotis*.

These plants thrive in a moist, gritty loam and partial shade.

Propagate from seed or root division. **Flowering** in spring.

Family AMARYLLIDACEAE *Narcissus* species

Known variously as daffodils, jonquils, chalice flowers, lent lilies and Chinese sacred lilies, the hardy bulbous perennials of this important genus come from Europe, Asia and North Africa. The leaves are narrow, linear and erect, varying in length according to species. The flowers may be borne singly or in numbers on a single stem. All narcissus are now classified into eleven divisions (sections), the first nine covering varieties of garden origin. Examples are: Div. I. Trumpet in which the corona or trumpet is as long as, or longer, than the perianth segments; Div. III. Small-cupped narcissi in which the cup or corona is not more than one-third the length of the perianth segments; one flower only to a stem; Div. IX. Poeticus narcissi. Characteristics of the narcissus poeticus group without admixture of any other, e.g. pheasant's eye narcissus. Div. X. species and wild forms and hybrids, i.e. all species and wild or reputedly wild forms and hybrids. Into this group come the dwarf-growing *N. cyclamineus* and *N. bulbocodium.*

Daffodils may be widely used for beds and borders, but are often best when naturalized. Well-drained loamy soils are best, planting by the end of August.

Propagate by offsets or from seeds. **Flowering** from March to May.

Family SCROPHULARIACEAE *Nemesia* species

Colourful half-hardy annuals from South Africa. *N. strumosa* is the most noteworthy species, reaching a height of 30 cm or more with 7·5 cm lace-shaped leaves and two-lipped flowers, of white, yellow or purple with a bearded throat of yellow heavily spotted. There are dwarf strains, including 'Blue Gem' and 'Triumph', the latter mixed-colours; very useful for massed effect. *N. floribunda*, 30 cm, bears spurred flowers, white or pale pink in colour, on many-flowered racemes; and *N. versicolor*, about 23 cm high, has spurred flowers usually two-coloured. From *N. versicolor* and *N. strumosa* various colour forms and strains have originated; 'Suttonii' is a good large-flowered mixed colour strain. Seed is sown in gentle heat in March, and the seedlings pricked off into boxes to be ready for planting out in May. Seed may also be sown out of doors in May to flower in August and September. Nemesias also are attractive pot plants if raised from seed sown in August and potted into 10-cm pots at Michaelmas to flower in winter.

Propagate from seed. **Flowering** from late June to Michaelmas.

Family Labiatae *Nepeta* species

A genus of about 150 species, widely distributed in the Northern Hemisphere, herbaceous perennials or annuals with aromatic, toothed, incised, opposite leaves. The flowers are tubular and small, and borne on stems up to a metre in height, white, blue or lavender shades. The common catmint of gardens is *N.* × *faassenii*, a hybrid derived from *N. mussinii* and commonly known as *N. mussinii* in gardens: 30 cm high, it is excellent for edging borders. Other good border plants are *N. mussinii* 'Superba' with dark lavender flowers and reaching a height of a metre, and the hybrid 'Six Hills Giant' which is very similar. *N. hederaceae* is the ground ivy of America and has a creeping habit. *N. macrantha*, 60 to 90 cm, is a silver-blue flowering species from Siberia. *N. nervosa*, from Kashmir, has clear blue flowers; height 38 cm.

They will grow freely in any good garden soil, preferring sun to shade. Planting may take place in early autumn or spring.

Propagate by division of the root in spring or by partly ripened tips taken as cuttings. **Flowering** throughout the summer.

Tobacco Plant A

Family SOLANACEAE *Nicotiana alata* var. *grandiflora*

Of these showy and fragrant perennials, best treated as half-hardy annuals, this is the best known, being a native of Brazil, and sometimes offered in seedsmen's catalogues under *N.* × *affinis*. The basal leaves are wide, like those of some mulleins, and from these the stems rise 1 to 1·5 metres, bearing a number of tubular flowers of elegant form, widening at the mouth with five petioles that are white in the type with a reverse of pale violet. There are also various forms with flowers of rose, crimson, pink, lilac and cream. Notable varieties are 'Crimson King', 60 to 90 cm; 'Lime Green', 70 cm; 'Daylight', white, 70 cm, remaining open during the day; 'Dwarf Idol', a crimson-flowered dwarf strain, 30 cm high. Cultivated both for the beauty of the flowers and for their fragrance, plants may be raised from seeds sown in gentle heat early in the year, pricked off into boxes, and planted out in late May. There are a number of other annual species, but this is by far the most favoured. A deep, moist soil is preferred; sun or shade.

Propagate from seed. **Flowering** season is in late summer.

Love-in-a-Mist

Family RANUNCULACEAE *Nigella damascena*

Also known as fennel-flower and a native of south-eastern Europe. The plant owes its name to the thread-like leaves that clothe the stems in a fern-like fashion and surround the flowers. The flowers are about 37 mm across, rounded and not unlike corn-flowers in form, being white, rose-red, blue or purple in colour. The blue-flowered varieties are the most desirable and the semi-double variety 'Miss Jekyll' is often grown to the exclusion of others, but 'Persian Rose', pale-pink, and 'Persian Jewels', a mixed colour strain 38 cm tall, are becoming increasingly popular. The Spanish species *N. hispanica* is more coarse in foliage and has flowers of blue with red stamens, up to 6·2 cm across, borne singly or in pairs. There are also white and purple forms.

Sow the seed outdoors in autumn or in March where the plants are to flower and allow the seedlings ample space for development. Full sun is essential and the soil must be rich in humus.

Propagation is from seed. **Flowering** from June to Michaelmas.

Evening Primrose **P B A**

Family ONAGRACEAE *Oenothera* species

An attractive group of hardy annuals, biennials and perennials from the Americas. Among the biennials *O. biennis*, North America, grows to 1·5 metres, bearing yellow flowers, which open late in the day. *O erythrosepala* (syn. *O. lamarckiana*) has larger, golden-yellow flowers; its form 'Afterglow' is noted for its red calyces. Among the annuals is the Californian *O. bistorta* with yellow and red, four-petalled flowers, 2·5. cm across, spotted red at the base, opening in the daytime. *O. odorata*, 30 to 60 cm from Chile, with yellow flowers fading to red before falling, is perennial. 'Fireworks', 45 cm high, is of garden origin. It has attractive red buds followed by bright yellow flowers. Only 15 cm high, *O. trichocalyx* usually dies after flowering. *O. fruticosa*, known as sundrops, is a perennial with golden yellow flowers about 5 cm across.

Sow the seeds in April in a sunny, well-drained position and thin the seedlings to 15 cm apart, or under glass in March for early flowering.

Propagation is from seed. **Flowering** from midsummer onwards.

Family Ranunculaceae *Paeonia* species

A genus of mainly Asiatic origin and many garden varieties. The flowers vary in size and may be of single or double form. *P. officinalis* is a long-established garden flower with 20-cm flowers of crimson on 60- to 90-cm stems. *P. tenuifolia* is a miniature form with double crimson flowers. *P. mlokosewitschii* has sulphur-yellow single flowers. *P. lactiflora* (syn. *P. albiflora*) is the origin of many of the beautiful garden varieties; reaches 90 cm with double flowers. *P. lutea*, shrubby, 90 cm from Yunnan, and *P. wittmanniana*, 60 cm, from the Orient, are good yellow-flowering species. *P. suffruticosa* (syn. P. *moutan*) is the tree paeony, 1 to 2 metres tall, with rose flowers. There are numerous colour forms and named varieties, both single and double-flowered.

Paeonies of all kinds should be planted in September or October. A deep soil rich in humus and a position in full sun is essential, as well as ample moisture but perfect drainage during growth.

Propagate by division in October or from seed. **Flowering** in May and June.

Iceland Poppy A

Family Papaveraceae *Papaver* species

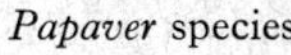

This family includes many annuals from Europe, Asia, North Africa, western North America or the Arctic regions. *P. nudicaule*, the Iceland poppy with flowers 7·5 cm or more across of white, yellow, pink, salmon and orange, has given rise to a number of well-known strains of garden origin, notably the 'Coonara', 'Gartref', and 'Kelmscott'. *P. nudicaule* is strictly a perennial, but is best treated as an annual. The opium poppy is *P. somniferum*, of Europe and Asia, with flowers of double and single form with frilled petals, that vary from white to red and purple. *P. rhoeas* is the corn poppy, native to Britain, with scarlet flowers, and is parent to a host of varieties, double, semi-double and single-flowered, of which the 'Shirley Poppy Strain' is most popular. There are also the scarlet *P. californicum*; *P. glaucum*, from Syria, with scarlet flowers, spotted purple at the base and *P. commutatum*, from Asia Minor, scarlet with a large black spot on each petal.

Propagation. Seed may be sown in spring or autumn where the plants are to flower.

Flowering from June to September.

Family PAPAVERACEAE *Papaver orientale*

A brilliantly coloured perennial, native to Asia Minor, and possessing the largest flowers of the genus. The leaves are deeply lobed and bristly, often 15 cm across. The stems are also bristly and attain heights varying from 1 to 1·2 metres though some of the garden forms are of a dwarf habit. The flowers are usually of six petals, broad and overlapping, of a brilliant orange-scarlet, with a deep purple base.

There is a wide range of variation in colour in the various forms of garden origin, good forms including 'Perry's White', 'Salmon Glow', 'Lord Lambourne', orange-scarlet, 'Beauty of Livermore', bright crimson-red, 'Watermelon', cherry-rose, 'Marcus Perry', orange-scarlet, 'Mrs. Perry', salmon-pink and 'Storm Torch', orange-red.

These plants will grow in any good deep garden soil and will remain in perfect vigour if allowed to remain undisturbed for several years to form large floriferous clumps.

Propagation is effected by root cuttings and from seed. **Flowering** late May and June.

Zonal Pelargonium

Family GERANIACEAE *Pelargonium* (forms of garden origin)

Popularly but erroneously known as geranium, the zonal pelargoniums of gardens are thought to be hybrids of the two South African species *P. zonale* and *P. inquinans*. These plants are of succulent growth and attain heights of 60 cm or more. The leaves are round, 7·5 to 12·7 cm across, scalloped and toothed, with a dark zone at the centre, and aromatic when crushed; the flowers are mostly single, 2·5 cm or more across and are borne in many-flowered umbels, the colours varying from orange-scarlet, pink and salmon to white. There are several thousand varieties in cultivation; dwarf, variegated and aromatic-leaved forms amongst them, including ivy-leafed forms (forms or hybrids of *P. peltatum*).

The best plants are obtained from cuttings rooted in the autumn for planting out in the following spring when all risk of frost has passed. The site chosen must be sunny and the soil humus-rich. Seedlings raised from seed sown as soon as it is ripe, in August, will bloom in ten months if grown on under heat in a greenhouse.

Propagation is from cuttings or seed. **Flowering** in summer.

Family SCROPHULARIACEAE *Penstemon* species

A genus of attractive perennials, largely for the herbaceous border, natives of North America. *P. barbatus* (syn. *Chelone barbata*) has numerous rosy-red tubular flowers, 2·5 cm long, each with a beard on the lower lip. 'Alice Hindley', lavender, 'Evelyn', pink, and 'Southgate Gem', bright red, are good forms. *P. campanulatus* has a free-branching habit, with one-sided racemes of rose-pink flowers. *P. ovatus* will reach 60 to 90 cm with flowers, about 19 mm long, of bright blue fading to purple. *P. antirrhinoides*, 30 to 90 cm, lemon-yellow, *P. diffusus*, light purple, and its white form, and *P. glaber*, 30 to 60 cm, purple, are all worth growing. *P. hartwegii*, usually grown as a biennial, has large tubular flowers of a bright scarlet. The hybrids 'Schonholzeri', bright red, 'Ruby', 'Crimson' and 'Garnet', originating from *P. hartwegii*, are all good border plants.

Sunny position and a well-drained rich loam, containing plenty of humus, are the essentials. Most have no great hardiness and cuttings should be taken and rooted in late summer, overwintering in a frost-free frame.

Propagate from cuttings or seed. **Flowering** in summer and autumn.

Family SOLANACEAE *Petunia hybrida*

The half-hardy perennial varieties are often grown as annuals and are hybrids between the Argentine species *P. nyctaginiflora* and *P. violacea*. The stems are leafy and attain a height of 30 cm or more, bearing many tubular flowers, 7·5 cm or more across at the mouth, of varied colours, purple, violet-blue, rose, crimson, white and striped bicolours. There are numerous strains, including dwarfer bedding varieties, a strain with trailing habit ideal for window boxes and strains with large frilled flowers, veined and blotched in the throat. Some strains have small single flowers, others large double flowers. Seed should be sown under glass in late January to March, care being taken to sow it thinly to avoid damping off. The seedlings are potted when 2·5 cm or so high, and it is important to avoid over-watering. Planting out of doors where the plants are to bloom may be carried out in early June when all risk of frost has passed.

Propagation is from seed, or cuttings taken in August. **Flowering** from late June to September.

Family HYDROPHYLLACEAE

Phacelia campanularia

Among the numerous species of this genus, the hardy Californian annuals are particularly favoured in flower gardens. In *P. campanularia* the leaves are ovate and toothed and the stems rise to 20 cm, bearing several intense blue flowers of bell shape. A valuable annual for a late spring sowing, flowering within six to eight weeks of germination. *P. tanacetifolia* is distinct, having clustered heads of small lavender or blue flowers on stems up to 90 cm in height. Other species occasionally encountered: *P. minor*, (syn. *P. whitlavia*), 30 cm, is the Californian bluebell, with blue or purple flowers. The form 'Alba' has white flowers. *P. ciliata* has fragrant, pretty lavender-bue flowers and grows 30 cm high. *P. viscida* (syn. *Eutoca viscida*) reaches 30 to 60 cm, with small flowers of bright blue with purple or white centres, particularly attractive to bees. A deeper tone of violet-blue is seen in the large-flowered *P. parryi*.

Easily raised by sowing seed in April in well-drained soil where the plants are to flower.

Propagation is from seed. **Flowering** from late June to Michaelmas.

Family POLEMONIACEAE *Phlox* species

One of the most brilliantly coloured genera, native to North America, containing annual, perennial and alpine species. *P. paniculata* (syn. *P. decussata*) has oblong, lance-shaped leaves and many flowers, from 2·5 to 5 cm across, borne in massive pyramidal panicles on stems up to 1·2 metres high. The colour of the many garden varieties varies from white to shades of pink, mauve, violet, purple, scarlet and crimson. *P. maculata*, 60 cm, has purple flowers, 'Alpha', clear pink and 'Miss Lingard', pure white, are amongst the best forms.

A deep, rich, gritty soil, well drained and sunny, is necessary for phlox to grow really well, although partial shade is advantageous for those of orange tones that tend to burn in the sun.

From the annual *P. drummondii* have arisen two basic types, 'Grandiflora', 25 to 30 cm, and 'Nana Compacta', 15 to 20 cm. They are found in a wide range of colour.

Propagate from root cuttings, top cuttings or seed.
Flowering from late June until September.

Family SOLANACEAE *Physalis* species

A race of about 100 species of annual and perennial plants, mostly from America but some from Europe and Asia. The leaves are rounded, serrated at the edge and pointed. *P. alkekengi*, known as winter cherry, Chinese lantern, bladder herb and strawberry tomato, is a perennial species from southern and eastern Europe. It reaches a height of about 30 cm with small white flowers and yellow anthers, followed by red cherry-like fruit enclosed in orange-red calyces of lantern-like appearance. *P. franchetii*, a native of Japan, is similar to the foregoing species but has larger calyces, 5 cm in diameter, and reaches 45 to 75 cm. It has been described as annual and biennial, but is perennial. *P.* × *bunyardi* is a hybrid form, with characteristics intermediate between the parents, *P. alkekengi* and *franchetii*. These plants are of little garden value, their main merit being their usefulness for winter adornment after the stems have been cut and dried. Will grow anywhere in drained soil.

Propagate by division or from seed. **Flowering** in summer and the calyces colour in late summer and autumn.

Family POLEMONIACEAE *Polemonium* species

P. coeruleum from the copses and margins of European streams is the old-fashioned species to which the genus owes its popular name from the manner in which the leaflets are arranged on the stem to suggest a ladder. It is also called Greek valerian. The plant reaches 60 cm and bears a short panicle of blue, drooping, bell-shaped flowers 2·5 cm across. The finest form is *P. lanatum* var. *humile* (syn. *P. richardsonii*) from North America, with bell-shaped flowers of brilliant blue and white anthers. 'Sapphire' is a light blue form. *P. pulcherrimum* has smaller flowers that vary in tone from violet to lavender-blue. *P. reptans*, a native of North America, is 15 cm high, with light blue flowers, 12 mm across, borne in a cluster. 'Blue Pearl' is a good form. *P. foliosissimum*, reaching 75 cm, has blue, narrowly bell-shaped flowers.

A position in partial shade and a deep rich soil is necessary to grow these plants to perfection and, when established, they may remain for many years without disturbance.

Propagate by division or from seed. **Flowering** in spring.

Family LILIACEAE *Polygonatum* species

A genus comprising about sixty species, well distributed over the temperate regions of the northern hemisphere. Of graceful habit, a number are worthy additions to the flower border. *P. multiflorum* has gracefully arching stems up to 90 cm high, the exterior clothed its entire length with elegant oblong leaves, 10 to 12 cm long, beneath which hang the drooping tubular flowers of white, about 2·5 cm long. It is a native of Europe and Asia. There are a number of forms and it is thought *P. multiflorum* may in fact be a hybrid. *P.* × *hybridum*, from the cross *P. multiflorum* × *P. odoratum*, is a better, more robust plant, valuable for shady situations. *P. japonicum* 'Variegatum', of moderate height, has green and white variegated leaves. *P. hookeri*, native to China and Tibet, is a dwarf species, 7 to 10 cm high, with solitary, scented, lilac-purple flowers. *P. verticillatum* carries its leaves in whorls, with flowers of greenish-white borne in bunches of three in the leaf axils; they are followed by red fruit.

Propagate by division or from seed. **Flowering** in spring.

Family PORTULACACEAE *Portulaca grandiflora*

A half-hardy annual from Brazil, known as the sun plant or rose moss. Of semi-prostrate habit, the plant grows 15 to 22 cm high. The leaves are fleshy and the flowers, borne at the ends of the stems, are 2·5 cm or more across and noted for their brilliance of colouring, which ranges from white and yellow to pink, scarlet, purple and crimson. There are several varieties and strains including double-flowered strains.

The plant is only suitable for a warm situation where it is fully exposed to the sun, such as a sunny, south or south-west facing bank or wall-side border; the soil must be well drained. Like the zinnia, the sun plant gives of its best in a hot and dry summer.

Inasmuch as the seedlings do not transplant well, it is best to sow the seed out of doors where the seedlings are to flower, under cloches, in April, giving protection until early June.

Propagation is from seed. **Flowering** from July to October.

Family Rosaceae *Potentilla* species

A genus comprising both shrubby and herbaceous perennials of eminent value as garden plants. The foliage is elegant and strongly resembles that of the strawberry, although in many species it is more finely divided. The hybrids have a long season of flowering and comprise many brilliant colours inherited from the species that were their parents. *P. argyrophylla* has erect stems, 60 to 90 cm high, with yellow flowers 2·5 cm across, borne on long pedicels. It is a native of the Himalayas, and has been hybridized with *P. atrosanguinea*, purple, *P. nepalensis*, rosy-purple, and possibly *P. villosa*, golden yellow, to produce the numerous garden hybrids which include varieties with double as well as single flowers in form like those of the strawberry, but with a colour variation that ranges from white and yellow to shades of buff, salmon, clear rose and scarlet. Among the best are the popular 'Gibson's Scarlet', single red, 'Miss Wilmott', cherry red, and 'Wm. Rollinson', dark orange. Easily grown in well-drained sandy soil in full sun.

Propagate by division or from seed. **Flowering** throughout the summer.

Family PRIMULACEAE *Primula* species

A genus of over 500 species containing many choice subjects for rock garden, flower border and woodland, native to Europe and Asia. Of the many species, there are certain ones that are common to gardens. *P. vulgaris* is the well-known European primrose, with flowers of yellow, purple or blue, each with a yellow centre. The polyanthus primrose, *P.* × *variabilis*, is of garden origin, from crosses between *P. vulgaris*, *P. veris* (cowslip) and possibly other species, and bears its flowers in clusters on erect stems. *P. juliae* is like a smaller *P. vulgaris*, purple in colour. *P. japonica* and *P. pulverulenta* bear their flowers, of a great variation in colour, in majestic candelabra fashion. *P. helodoxa*, a yellow-flowered Candelabra type, reaches 90 cm in height. *P. auricula* is an old florist's flower, and the named varieties, both show and alpine, are best grown in pots in a frame or cold greenhouse where the lovely purple, red, yellow, grey and green edged forms are a delight.

There are some excellent strains such as 'Pacific Giant' hybrids which may be grown from seed in partially shaded positions where there is ample humus.

Propagate by division or from seed. **Flowering** in spring.

Family COMPOSITAE *Pyrethrum roseum*

Known to gardeners as *Pyrethrum roseum*, the botanically correct name of this plant, from which originated the colourful spring-flowering pyrethrums, is *Chrysanthemum coccineum*. It is a perennial, native to Persia and the Caucasus. The foliage is finely cut and fern-like in appearance, forming a thick mass from which rise stems to a height of 60 to 90 cm, bearing flowers 5 cm or more across of white, red, rose or lilac shades. The species is rarely seen, having long given place to the many fine varieties of garden origin that comprise both double and single flowered varieties ranging through pink, salmon, scarlet, crimson and wine-red tones. The single-flowered forms are effectively centred with an orange, yellow or cream disc. For massing in the herbaceous border and for cutting, this plant is most valuable, and great quantities are grown annually for the flower market. *Chrysanthemum uliginosum* (*P. uliginosum*) is a tall white-flowered plant, very like a Michaelmas daisy in appearance and flowering in September.

Easily grown in any well-drained soil.

Propagate by division before or immediately after flowering, or from seed. **Flowering** in June.

Family RANUNCULACEAE *Ranunculus* species

A genus of several hundred species found throughout the world. *R. asiaticus*, or turban buttercup, is an old garden favourite, 30 cm high, with elegantly cut foliage and double yellow flowers, 37 mm across. From this species come the garden varieties known as Turkish, with orange, yellow or purple flowers; Persian, with double and single flowers of every shade except blue. This is a species with tuberous roots, comprising claw-like fangs that are placed facing downwards when planting. *R. aconitifolius* 'Plenus', known as fair maids of France, is densely covered with small white flowers of rosette-like form. *R. acris* 'Flore-pleno', the batchelor's button, will attain 60 cm, with button-like rosettes of rich yellow. *R. amplexicaulis*, 15 to 30 cm high, has single flowers of white. *R. montanus* is a charming plant of easy cultivation with a wealth of large flowers on 10-cm stems. It requires alpine garden conditions. The tuberous-rooted kinds demand a sandy soil, rich in humus and moist. Plant December to April.

Propagate tuberous-rooted species by offsets and the remainder by division. **Flowering** from April to September.

Mignonette

Family Resedaceae

Reseda odorata

For long a cherished favourite in British gardens and a native of North Africa and Egypt. The plant, familiar to all who visit gardens, is a perennial, treated as an annual. Of upright growth at first, it tends to a spreading and decumbent habit, with leafy stems and trusses of many small yellowish-white flowers of delightful and pronounced fragrance. There are a number of garden forms with flowers of red and yellow, sulphur, golden yellow and orange. Good named forms include, 'Giant Machet', pale red, 25 cm, 'Red Monarch', dark red, 30 cm, 'Goliath', double-flowered, red, 45 cm. The spikes of these garden varieties are invariably much larger than those of the type. *R. luteola*, a native species, is sometimes grown for cutting. Choose a sunny position and well-drained soil, and sow the seed out of doors in April where the plants are to bloom. When a few centimetres high, the seedlings should be thinned to 10 to 15 cm apart. Owing to the fineness of the seeds thin sowing is necessary. Mignonette may also be sown in autumn and protected by cloches if the weather is severe. The plants will flower earlier than those sown in the spring.

Propagation is from seed. **Flowering** from late June to Michaelmas.

Family PAPAVERACEAE *Romneya* species

A genus of two species of distinct and beautiful plants, native to California and hardy in most parts of Britain. *R. coulteri* is the best-known species, with elegantly cut poppy-like leaves, glaucose green and about 10 cm long. The fragrant flowers are like large single white poppies, about 15 cm across, with a bunch of yellow anthers at the centre; it will reach a height of 1·5 to 1·8 metres under good cultivation. *R. trichocalyx* is very similar but more erect and less branched. *R.* × *hybrida*, a hybrid between the two species, is the most free-flowering of the genus and the best garden plant.

A sunny sheltered position at the base of a south wall, where the soil is well drained and some protection may be given in severe winters, is ideal. Plants are usually cut back to near soil level in spring although perennial stems may develop in mild, relatively frost-free areas. The soil must be well drained and moderately rich in humus. Once established, the plants will not transplant satisfactorily and should be allowed to remain undisturbed. Plant from pots in spring.

Propagate by root cuttings or from seed. **Flowering** from June to September.

Family COMPOSITAE *Rudbeckia* species

This genus contains perennials and annuals, native to North America. *R. bicolor* is an annual with yellow-rayed flowers, 5 cm across, with maroon centres. There are several named forms. *R. hirta*, black-eyed Susan, is an annual or biennial with golden yellow-rayed flowers deepening at the base, where they merge into purplish-brown discs. Also annual or biennial, *R. triloba*, or brown-eyed Susan, reaches 90 cm to 1·2 metres, with flowers of yellow with orange or bronze-purple shading at the base and black central discs. There are several good hybrid annual strains. Perennials of garden origin include 'Goldquelle', chrome yellow, and 'Goldsturm', golden with black centre.

Propagation. In the case of biennials, seeds may be sown in late summer to provide plants that will flower in the following year. But it is more usual to sow them and the annual species under glass in March, the seedlings being pricked off and planted out where they are to flower in late May, or seeds may be sown where they are to flower in late April.

Flowering in late summer and early autumn.

Painted-tongue **A**

Family SOLANACEAE *Salpiglossis sinuata*

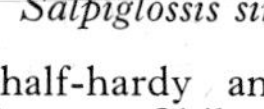

A half-hardy annual, native to Chile, that is quite distinctive in character. The plant is of elegant branching habit, growing 60 to 75 cm tall. The leaves are oblong, and the flowers are funnel-shaped with a wide throat. There are many garden strains and varieties in colours of primrose, scarlet, pink, yellow, etc., all attractively veined and mottled. The strain 'Emperor' (syn. var. *superbissima*) is non-branching and of a decided columnar character. 'Splash' is a compact strain, growing to about 45 cm with a wide range of brilliant colours. 'Bolero' is a good, large-flowered strain. For outdoor flowering, seed must be sown under glass, temperature 18° C to 23° C, in March, the seedlings being pricked off singly into 5-cm pots and planted out when large enough in early June, choosing a well-drained soil and a position in full sun. Seed may also be sown in August or September, under glass, and the seedlings grown on in pots for flowering in the following March or April.

Propagation is from seed. **Flowering** in April and May under glass and from June to September out of doors.

Sage

Family Labiatae

Salvia species

A genus that includes annuals, biennials and perennials grown as annuals. The biennial *S. sclarea* (syn. *S. bracteata*) is the clary, native to the Mediterranean, with broad leaves up to 22 cm long, with bracts of rose and white and bluish-white flowers, about 2·5 cm long, borne in branched racemes and 60 cm tall. *S. superba* (*S. nemorosa*), 1·2 metres, has brilliant purple flowers; a perennial species. *S. coccinea*, 60 to 90 cm, is a South America species, bearing deep scarlet flowers in autumn. *S. farinacea*, 60 to 90 cm, from Mexico, with lavender-blue flowers; *S. splendens*, 60 to 90 cm, of Brazil, the scarlet sage, are both popular grown as half-hardy annuals. There are numerous strains of *S. splendens*, flowers scarlet or purple. *S. sclarea*, being biennial, is best raised from seed sown in spring, planted out in permanent positions, when the plants are large enough, to flower in the following summer. *S. horminum*, a hardy annual, 45 cm, and its varieties are raised from seed sown in March where the plants are to flower, in warm sunny positions.

Flowering in summer.

Family CARYOPHYLLACEAE *Saponaria officinalis*

A genus of the pink family, comprising both annual and perennial herbs, a number being useful for the adornment of rock gardens and flower borders, inhabiting principally the Mediterranean region. *S. officinalis* is a pretty native plant, known as 'bouncing Bet' reaching 60 cm with lance-shaped leaves clothing the stems in clusters and rose-pink flowers about 2·5 cm or more across borne in a compact truss at the top portion of the stems, rather like *Phlox paniculata*. *S. officinalis*, 'Roseo Plena', is an attractive double form with pink or white flowers that is preferable to the type. There are various other forms showing slight variation in the depth of colour and mostly with double flowers.

Will grow in any well-drained soil in full sun or partial shade, and well able to fend for itself under wild garden conditions when well established. Useful for contrasting with *Scabiosa caucasica* and other perennials with light blue or lavender flowers.

Propagate by division in the spring, or by cuttings. **Flowering** from July to September.

Family DIPSACEAE *Scabiosa* species

Scabiosa caucasica, from the Caucasus, is the finest of the perennial species, reaching 90 cm in height, has lavender-blue flowers some 7 to 10 cm across. Usually represented in gardens by named forms, such as 'Clive Greaves', a good mid-blue; 'Moorheim's Blue', deep violet; 'Miss Wilmott', ivory white. *S. graminifolia*, with silvery, grass-like leaves and lilac-pink pincushion flowers, is about 30 cm in height.

Of the annual species, only *S. atropurpurea*, known as sweet scabious, and its various attractive strains, are widely grown. A native of south-west Europe, erect, growing to 90 cm in height, fragrant flowers, usually deep crimson. There is a wide range of colour in the named varieties and both tall and dwarf forms. Double-flowered strains include 'Cockade', mixed colours, and 'Rose Cockade', rose-pink.

Propagate annuals from seed; perennials by division. Perennials: plant in any ordinary well-drained soil, choosing a sunny situation. **Flowering** from July to September.

Family LILIACEAE *Scilla* species

A race of pretty bulbous plants, comprising about eighty species indigenous to the temperate regions of Europe, Asia and Africa. *S. hispanica* is the Spanish squill, with blue bell-shaped flowers in slender racemes on 45-cm stems. There are also pink and white forms. *S. peruviana*, the Cuban lily, a native of Algeria, has lilac-blue star-shaped flowers in dense conical clusters, sometimes 15 cm across. *S. siberica*, the well-known Siberian squill, reaches up to 15 cm with starry bell-shaped flowers that vary from pale to deep blue with a central line of dark blue to each segment; there is also a pure white form. Rather similar and also of easy cultivation is *S. tubergeniana*, with its rather flatter flowers, pale blue with a dark blue central stripe down each segment. *S. nutans* is the common bluebell of English woodland. There are a number of other species, all more or less attractive.

Easily grown in rich, well drained sandy soil in sun or partial shade. All are quite hardy, except *S. peruviana*, which needs some slight winter protection in severe localities. Effective for naturalizing in bold drifts in short grass.

Propagate by offsets or from seed. **Flowering** in February or March for *S. siberica* and *S. tubergeniana*, and in May and June for the others.

Stonecrop

Family CRASSULACEAE *Sedum spectabile*

The sedums are a race of succulents, mainly used in rock gardens but containing a few species or garden forms suitable for the flower border. *S. spectabile*, a species from Japan, has leaves that are rounded, fleshy, glaucous and 5 cm or more across. The flowers are about 12 mm across, bright pink in colour and are borne in flat clustered heads, up to 15 cm across, on 45-cm stems. There are a number of forms with deeper coloured flowers, among the best being 'Brilliant', deep pink, 'Carmen', carmine pink, 'Meteor', carmine red, and 'Autumn Joy', salmon-pink, tinged bronze. There is also a form with variegated foliage. *S. maximum* var. *atropurpureum*, 45 cm, has purple leaves and pink flowers.

These plants will thrive, like most succulents, in the hottest and driest of soils as well as in shade, and the foliage alone is an attractive foil to the brighter coloured perennials. When in bloom the flowers possess some attraction that causes them to receive the constant attention of butterflies.

Propagate by offsets and from seed. **Flowering** season is in late summer.

Golden Rod **P**

Family Compositae *Solidago* species

A genus with natives of North America and Europe that are mainstays of the late summer flower border. The plants are erect in habit with stems well clothed with leaves of oval, pointed character and heads of yellow feathery panicles, comprising many small flowers on arching stems, in effect not unlike a yellow astilbe. The species vary considerably from the tall *S. canadensis* with its panicles borne on 1·2- to 1·8-metre stems to *S. brachystachys*, a dwarf carpeter, 15 to 22 cm high. *S. virgaurea*, the native golden rod, 60 to 90 cm, with dense terminal heads, is with *S. canadensis*, the originator of a number of taller garden hybrids and, with *S. brachystachys*, of the newer dwarf hybrids. Good hybrid forms include 'Golden Thumb', 30 cm, a dwarf variety for the front of the border, 'Cloth of Gold', 45 cm, deep yellow, 'Crown of Rays', 60 cm, horizontal sprays of yellow flowers, 'Lemore', 60 cm, soft primrose yellow, 'Ballardii', up to 1·5 metres, rich golden yellow.

All may be grown easily in any good garden soil in full sun or semi-shade, and are useful as foils to the tall and dwarf blue and purple Michaelmas daisies.

Propagate by division and from seed. **Flowering** in late summer.

Family AMARYLLIDACEAE

Sternbergia lutea

A bulbous plant, native to the Mediterranean region, Syria and Iran. It is believed to be the lily-of-the-fields referred to in the New Testament, and has been in cultivation in Britain for more than three centuries; sometimes called winter daffodil. The tubular flowers are rather more than 5 cm in length, bright yellow and in shape rather like a crocus; they do not rise above the leaves, which are narrow and strap-shaped, about 30 cm long and 12 mm wide. *S. sicula* (syn. *S. lutea* var. *angustifolia*) is rather similar but with deeper flower colour and narrower leaves; var. *graeca* (syn. *S. lutea* var. *sicula*) has even narrower leaves. Of this small genus, *S. clusiana* has the largest flowers, up to 10 cm across, with flowers opening before the leaves.

Very effective when grown in bold masses in short turf and at the front of shrubberies or foot of a warm, sunny wall.

Easily grown in any well-drained, gritty soil. Plant 7·5 cm deep.

Propagate by means of offsets or from seed. **Flowering** in September and October.

French and African Marigold A

Family COMPOSITAE *Tagetes* species

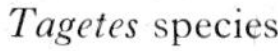

This is a genus of half-hardy annuals, mostly natives of Mexico, erroneously supposed to have originated in Africa. *T. erecta* is still called the African marigold: it is of upright growth of 60 to 90 cm with flowerheads of brilliant orange or yellow. The French marigold is *T. patula*, with finely divided fern-like leaves and flowers, 37 mm across, on 30- to 45-cm stems. The flowers of the type are brownish-yellow, marked red. Those of garden varieties may vary from yellow to orange, all with red, maroon or mahogany markings. Dwarf strains such as 'Dainty Marietta' and 'Golden Ball' are excellent for edging. *T. signata*, 30 to 45 cm, has finely cut leaves and solitary yellow flowers, 2·5 cm across. There are many named varieties, deservedly popular for their long period of flowering. Afro-French hybrids, of recent introduction, combine the best qualities of both types.

Although seed may be sown out of doors in April where the plants are to flower, the best flowers are produced from seedlings raised under glass from seed sown in March and planted out of doors in May.

Propagation is from seed. **Flowering** from late June to September.

Family RANUNCULACEAE *Thalictrum* species

A race of fine foliaged herbaceous plants, native to northern temperate regions and eminently suitable for flower borders. *T. minus* is very variable in form and has been widely distributed under various names. The form 'Adiantifolium' is attractive mainly for its foliage that resembles a miniature maidenhead fern up to 30 cm, the greenish-white flowers being insignificant from the point of view of garden effect. *T. aquilegifolium* reaches 90 cm, with larger foliage similar to that of the aquilegia, and flowers borne in elegant heads where the purple or pink stamens are numerous and conspicuous, giving an attractive fluffy appearance; there are various improved gardens forms. *T. dipterocarpum*, 1·2 to 1·5 metres in height, with deep lavender flowers, is one of the most attractive species. 'Alba' and 'Hewitt's Double' are good forms. *T. flavum* has yellow flowers.

Easily grown in any good soil that is well drained, rich in humus, in sun or partial shade.

Propagate by division or from seed. **Flowering** from June to August.

Thyme P

Family Labiatae *Thymus* species

A genus of over a hundred species, mostly native to temperate regions, particularly of the Mediterranean. Of the dwarf creeping species, *T. serpyllum*, 15 cm, with its small, green ovate foliage, about 12 mm long, and purple flowers, 6 mm long, is a very variable species with numerous named forms or varieties. Some may, strictly speaking, be forms of *T. drucei*, but are more usually found listed under *T. serpyllum*. They include 'Albus', white, 'Argenteus', silver variegated foliage, 'Aureus', yellow variegated foliage, 'Cinereus', lilac-purple flowers, 'Coccineus', taller, with crimson flowers and, particularly good forms, 'Annie Hall', pale pink, 'Bressingham', clear pink, and 'Pink Chintz', rose-pink; all have aromatic foliage. The lemon-scented thyme (*T. citriodorus*), 15 to 22 cm, with small leaves, lemon-scented, and pink flowers, has silver variegated and golden variegated varieties. *T.* × 'Porlock', 22 cm high, has grey-green foliage and deep pink flowers.

The thymes are easily grown in any well-drained soil, in the crevices between paving-stones, and particularly effective when used as carpeters for early spring-flowering bulbous subjects.

Propagate by division, layering, cuttings or from seed. **Flowering** from June to September.

Family IRIDACEAE *Tigridia pavonia*

Of the thirty or so species in the genus *Tigridia*, the only one frequently encountered is *T. pavonia*, a half-hardy bulbous plant from Mexico, also called tiger iris. The stems are forked and leafy, rising 30 to 60 cm, the plaited leaves being from 22 to 38 cm long. The flowers consist of three outer segments and three short inner ones with a violet base, changing to scarlet at the tips of the outer segments; it is the central zone of yellow blotched with purple that gives the flower its name. There are many beautiful forms, white with purple spotted centre; yellow with mottled centre; yellow with purple blotched centre, the various colour forms having in the past been given names but now usually sold as Mixed Colours. The individual flowers last only a day, but are followed by others.

May be grown in full sun, in well-drained rich soil. Plant in late March, 12 cm deep, and, if necessary, protect from late frosts by a light covering of bracken. Lift as soon as the foliage ripens in late summer, ripen the bulbs and store away from frost during winter.

Propagate by means of offsets or from seed. **Flowering** in summer.

Spider-wort **P**

Family Commelinaceae

Tradescantia virginiana

A genus containing both hardy and tender species, *T. virginiana* being the most favoured for gardens and a native of North America. It was named for John Tradescant, gardener to Charles I. The leaves are produced freely and are narrow and arching, forming a generous tuft from which the leaf-clad flower-stems rise to a height of 30 to 60 cm, carrying umbels of several flowers, 2·5 to 5 cm across, and of an attractive violet-blue colour that varies in depth. There are various forms, such as 'Alba', white, 'Atrosanguinea', dark red, 'Caerulea Flora-plena', violet blue, double-flowered, 'Coccinea', bright red, 'Violacea', purple-blue to violet. There are also a number of worthy garden forms of which 'J. C. Weguelin', of clear lavender-blue, 'Leonora' of rich violet-blue, 'Isis', deep blue, and 'Osprey', white with feathery blue stamens, are first class. A most accommodating plant in cultivation, thriving under dry as well as wet conditions and in sun or shade.

Propagate by division or from seed. **Flowering** from June until autumn.

Family RANUNCULACEAE *Trollius* species

Natives of the north temperate zone, where they inhabit moist or swampy places. The roots are thick and fibrous and the leaves are palmately lobed or divided. The stems are leafy, of variable stature, according to species, and bear up to fifteen sepals with numerous stamens in the centre. *T. europaeus* reaches 45 to 60 cm, with lemon-yellow flowers, 5 cm across. 'Superbus' is a good form. *T. asiaticus* is of similar height with orange flowers. These two with *T. chinensis* have been used to produce the many fine varieties of garden origin grouped under the name of *T.* × *cultorum.* Good hybrid forms include 'Goldquelle', buttercup yellow, 'Orange Princess', orange-yellow, 'First Lancers', deep orange, and 'Canary Bird', pale yellow. *T. ledebouri*, from Siberia, reaches 60 cm with orange flowers, and blooms after the other species. 'Golden Queen' is a good form.

Easily grown in any deep, moist, loamy soil in partially shaded borders or by ponds or streams and in a position where there is shade or moderate exposure to the sun. Excellent plants for the waterside.

Propagate by division or from seed. **Flowering** in May and June for *T. europaeus* and *T. asiaticus*, and later for *T. ledebouri*.

Family GERANIACEAE *Tropaeolum majus*

T. majus is strictly a perennial and native to Peru, but is cultivated in Britain as a hardy annual. The habit is climbing; the leaves are rounded and of kidney shape; the flowers are about 6 cm across, with nectary spurs. There are now many varieties, climbing and dwarf, single and double, with a colour range varying from yellow to shades of orange, yellow, pink and red. Some varieties have variegated leaves. The 'Gleam' strain is semi-dwarf, 'Jewel Mixture' a good double-flowered dwarf strain. 'Nanum' is the single dwarf Tom Thumb strain, comprising many varieties of low bushy growth. The Peruvian *T. peregrinum* is the familiar canary creeper with yellow flowers and of self-climbing habit. Seed of *T. majus* and varieties may be sown in April outdoors in a sunny situation and not too rich soil where the plants are to flower, being particularly useful for dry sunny banks. The seeds are used for salads. Seed of *T. peregrinum* may be sown under glass in March and planted in May.

Propagation is from seed. **Flowering** from July to September.

Family LILIACEAE *Tulipa* species

An invaluable genus of bulbous plants, native to Europe, North Africa and many parts of Asia. *T. gesneriana* is the name given to the very variable race of tulips introduced from Turkish gardens during the 16th century. From *T. gesneriana* have been derived many of the classes or divisions of modern garden tulips, e.g. Darwins, Rembrandts, Cottage, Parrot, Bijbloemen, Bizarre, Lily-flowered, etc., in an almost infinite range of colours and shapes, and innumerable varietal names. *T. suaveolens*, a fragrant, scarlet and orange, 15-cm tulip from the Crimea, is parent to some of the early flowering varieties. Species tulips are the wild tulips from abroad. *T. kaufmanniana*, the water lily tulip from Central Asia, 20 cm, with creamy-white flowers, striped rose on the back, has several distinguished varieties.

Plant in November in well-drained sandy loam, with bone meal, in full sun. Lift, dry and store when foliage has died down in early summer. Some of the species tulips may survive out of doors in a sunny well-drained border, but lifting is more reliable.

Propagate by offsets or from seeds. **Flowering** from March to May.

Family SCROPHULARIACEAE *Verbascum* species

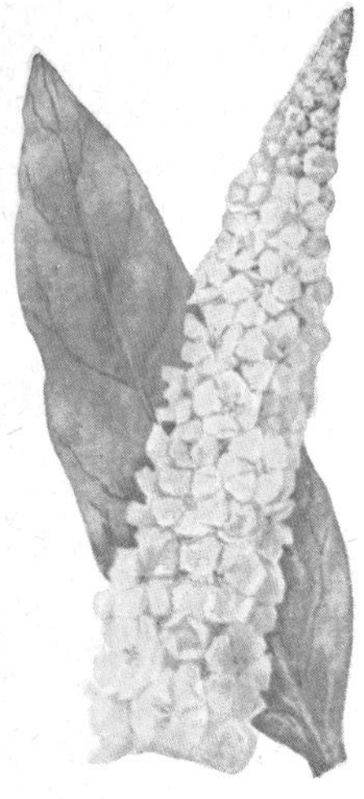

A genus of numerous species from Europe and the Mediterranean region. There are many that are useful for the flower garden, the following being the most usually cultivated. *V. nigrum* (syn. *V. vernale*), Britain, has long, broad leaves of felt-like texture, greyish-green in colour and well over 30 cm long. The stem attains 90 cm to 1·2 metres, and the upper portion consists of a number of ascending branches bearing closely together small yellow flowers, each with a purple centre. *V. chaixii*, the nettle-leaved mullein, has foliage 15 cm long, green covered with white tomentum; the flowers are yellow, with purple stamens and borne in racemes, 90 cm tall. There is a white form. *V. longifolia* has huge leaves, 60 cm long, attains 1·2 metres, and bears bright yellow flowers, 2·5 cm across, in a dense raceme. There are a number of named hybrids e.g., 'Pink Domino', rose-pink, 'Miss Wilmott', white, 'Golden Bush', rounded, bushy, long-flowering, 'Letitia', dwarf, about 30 cm high. Easily grown in good well-drained soil where lime is present and with a position in full sun. Not long lived.

Propagate by root cuttings or from seed. **Flowering** in June and July.

Family VERBENACEAE *Verbena* species

Hardy and half-hardy perennials, usually grown in Britain as annuals. The leaves are of a soft texture, oblong, 5 to 7·5 cm in length, and notched; the flowers are borne on 22- to 30-cm stems and form a broad corymb, 5 to 7·5 cm long, of white, yellow, pink or red colouring. *V.* × *hybrida* is believed to be a multiple hybrid of garden origin. There are numerous named strains. *V. canadensis* is the clump verbena with branching stems to 45 cm, with heads of reddish-purple, lilac, rose or white flowers; there are improved forms of garden origin. *V. rigida* (*V. venosa*) violet-purple flowers, up to 60 cm high, is very effective grown with yellow marigolds; has tuberous roots and is reasonably hardy in milder areas. *V. bonariensis*, purple, up to 45 cm, is excellent for cutting. A useful genus for massed effect and easily raised from seed sown under glass in March, and the seedlings pricked off and planted out of doors in May, or early June. It is also practicable to sow out of doors in May for flowering in late summer.

Propagation is from seed, or from cuttings overwintered in greenhouse or frame. **Flowering** from July to September.

Family SCROPHULARIACEAE *Veronica* species

Also called bird's eye, a genus of annual, perennial and shrubby species from Europe, America and New Zealand. Of the perennial types there are several attractive species. *V. longifolia* reaches 45 to 60 cm, with flowers lilac in colour and borne in a dense raceme. 'Foerster's Blue', is a good, strong, deep blue form. *V. spicata* reaches 45 to 60 cm; the flowers are small, mostly blue and borne in lengthy dense racemes. Of its forms the following are particularly attractive: 'Alba', white, 'Pavane', pink with grey foliage, and 'Baccarole', deep pink. *V. gentianoides* (syn. *V. glabra*) reaches 20 to 30 cm, with pale blue flowers. *V. teucrium*, has slender lavender blue spikes up to 60 cm high, 'Crater Lake Blue', vivid blue, 'Shirley Blue', bright blue, 22 cm, and 'Royal Blue', are good forms. *V. incana*, a native of Russia, has dark blue flowers; 'Wendy', a good form, has lavender-blue flowers and greyish foliage. Easily grown in any well-drained soil.

Propagate by division or from seed. **Flowering** season is in spring and summer.

Family VIOLACEAE *Viola* species

A race of dainty perennials that inhabit the temperate regions of the Old and New Worlds. *V. cornuta*, or the horned violet, has rounded foliage, toothed and of tufted habit; the flowers, 5 cm or less at the widest part, are violet. Its forms show a great variation in colour from white to yellow and purple, and was used extensively by raisers when evolving the brilliantly coloured bedding tufted pansies or violas of which there are numerous named varieties and mixed strains. Usually treated as annuals or biennials and referred to as *Viola* × *hybrida* or pansy. *V. odorata* is the favourite sweet-scented violet with its many shades of colour and with double and single flowers. 'Marie Louise', 'Princess of Wales', and 'Czar' are amongst the best of the varieties still in cultivation.

A position in partial shade is preferable and in soil that has been enriched with a liberal quantity of leaf-mould or old manure, moisture with good drainage being essential to their well-being. *V. odorata* and forms are best given frame protection in winter.

Propagate by means of cuttings or from seed.
Flowering in spring and summer.

Family Compositae *Zinnia elegans*

Known in its country of origin, Mexico, as youth and old age. An annual of upright habit with stems that rise to 75 cm with daisy-like flowers, 11 cm across. The double-flowered varieties of garden origin possess a wide range of colours that may vary from white to yellow, orange, scarlet, crimson and almost every conceivable shade except blue. There are many varieties in distinct types, e.g., 'Lilliput', 'Giant Dahlia-flowered', etc. *Z. haageana*, of tropical America, has orange-scarlet flowers of single form. Good strains include 'Persian Carpet', with bicolour flowers, 30 cm, 'Peter Pan', large flowers in various colours on bushy, 15-cm plants, 'Thumbelina', doubles and semi-doubles in a wide range of colours, 15 cm.

It is only in a really hot summer that zinnias can be relied upon to give of their best in Britain. Seed may be sown in a house or cold frame in mid-March, and the seedlings potted as soon as the first pair of natural leaves appear, and planted out in mid-May. Zinnias need a sunny position and a deep, humus-rich, well-drained soil.

Propagation is from seed. **Flowering** from late July until frost.

INDEX